FAMILY WALKS IN Perth OUTDOORS

DEPARTMENT OF CONSERVATION AND LAND MANAGEMENT

Published by: Dr Syd Shea, Executive Director, Department of Conservation and Land Management, 50 Hayman Road, Como, Western Australia 6152.
Executive Editor: Ron Kawalilak
Managing Editor: Ray Bailey
Editor and Compiler: David Gough
Features: John Hunter and David Gough
Design and Production: Sue Marais
Cover Photography: Robert Garvey
Illustrations and Location Maps: Gooitzen van der Meer
Mud Maps*: Sandra Van Brugge
Marketing: Estelle de San Miguel
Printed in Western Australia by: Scott Four Colour

*The mud maps and text are based on information provided by CALM staff and volunteers.

Acknowledgements:
To the many CALM staff in the Swan Region; the staff of Whiteman Park; the Friends of Star Swamp, particularly David Pike; the Friends of Trigg Bushland Reserve, particularly Steve Tulip; and the many volunteers, including friends and relatives, who took time to walk and describe each of the walks contained in this book.
To St John Ambulance Australia for First Aid information.
To Bob Cooper Outdoor Education for bushcraft and safety information.
Thank you all for your support in this project.

© 1993. ISBN 0-7309-6108-7

 Department of Conservation and Land Management

Foreword

Welcome to the first volume of *Family Walks in Perth Outdoors*.

Family Walks in Perth Outdoors contains 52 walks, one for every week of the year. The walks are ideal for families and most of them can be completed in a couple of hours. They are intended to provide interest, variety and exercise, while informing you about your natural surroundings.

This book complements *Perth Outdoors: A Guide to Natural Recreation Areas in and around Perth* and, like that popular publication, it is aimed at helping and encouraging WA's residents and visitors alike to enjoy the State's wonderful natural assets.

Syd Shea

EXECUTIVE DIRECTOR
Department of Conservation and Land Management

AUSTRALIAN ADMIRAL

Contents

INTRODUCTION

FAMILY WALKS IN PERTH OUTDOORS

FEATURES

INDEXES

Introduction

ABOUT THIS BOOK

Family Walks in Perth Outdoors is designed to complement CALM's best selling book *Perth Outdoors: A Guide to Natural Recreation Areas in and around Perth*. The 52 walks described in this book are listed first by geographical location (Hills, North, River and South) and then alphabetically by name within those regions. This is a similar structure to the book *Perth Outdoors*. Each walk is also numbered and this number is used in the various indexes at the back of the book. There are three indexes: alphabetical, by length and by ecosystem (see the section 'Walking in Perth Outdoors' on page 8).

Each walk has a mud map and a description of some of things you might see along the way. The majority of walks have carparks and picnic facilities at the start or nearby. Some have toilets, water and other facilities.

Distances and travelling times from Perth GPO are approximate and walk times are based on taking a leisurely stroll rather than a brisk walk.

The walk grades are given only as a guide to how difficult or strenuous each walk might be and do not reflect how safe it is. They are as follows:

❖ Grade 1 - Short, easy walks suitable for people of all ages and fitness levels.
❖ Grade 2 - As Grade 1, but longer than about three kilometres.
❖ Grade 3 - Suitable for people with a moderate level of fitness and will generally be longer than about three kilometres.
❖ Grade 4 - As Grade 3, but will have steps or short uneven stretches that may be loose or slippery underfoot.
❖ Grade 5 - Long or strenuous walks for experienced or fit walkers. Trails may be unmarked and go over steep, slippery or uneven surfaces.

While every effort has been made to ensure that the information provided in this book is accurate, no responsibility can be taken for any changes made since the walks were surveyed, or for the state of repair of any walk, as this is subject to weather and usage. When walking in the bush or along established trails, it is important to tread carefully and keep an eye open for potential hazards.

Your safety is our concern, but your responsibility.

WALKING IN PERTH OUTDOORS

Walking through natural bushland is a pleasurable experience. To be surrounded by the sounds, colours, smells and different types of life forms in and around Perth is both enlightening and exhilarating. Few capital cities are blessed with such a variety of natural areas right on their doorsteps.

The natural environment of Perth is made up of four distinctive natural communities, or ecosystems:

- ❖ the forests and woodlands of the Darling Range and Scarp;
- ❖ the woodlands of the Coastal Plain;
- ❖ the wetlands of lakes, streams, rivers and estuaries; and
- ❖ the coast and marine environments.

These distinctive natural communities are characterised by the soil type, landform and dominant plant life. The plants, animals, insects and other invertebrates, micro-organisms, rocks, soil, water, aspect to the sun and resultant microclimate all combine in subtle ways within each community to make each walk different. Wherever you choose to walk within a natural community you can see both the common and specific characteristics that make each place special.

The 52 family walks in this book are also indexed according to the natural communities or ecosystems through which they pass.

The Forests and Woodlands of the Darling Range and Scarp

The Darling Range is the tilted edge of a huge plateau that is the foundation of this part of Western Australia. Here, some of the oldest rocks on Earth are exposed. The granites, gneisses and quartzites are more than 2 500 million years old.

The overlying mantle of orange-red laterite rock formed about 10 million years ago, when wetter and more humid conditions than those of today leached minerals from the soil to form and insoluble hard crust. Jarrah trees, with their stringy grey-black bark, are predominant. Jarrah forest, with its low understorey of wildflowers and groves of grass trees, is a definitive image of the Darling Range, particularly when back-lit by the sun in the early morning and late afternoon.

The western extremity of the Darling Range is the Darling Scarp. Standing 200 metres or so above the coastal plain, it is the distinctive feature of the Perth horizon. The scarp exposes huge granite rocks and favours white-trunked wandoo trees.

The Woodlands of the Coastal Plain

The forested foothills below the Darling Scarp spill onto the coastal plain. Here the less fertile sands support woodlands of banksia, sheoaks, stunted eucalypts of jarrah and marri, and, where creamy-grey limestone is exposed, groves of tuart.

Shrublands and wildflower heathlands form the understorey. In the wetter areas, paperbarks proliferate. Without landform features, we most often take these woodlands for granted. In spring and early summer the trees, shrubs and heathlands display their presence with a profusion of flowers.

A complex of sand dune systems is aligned roughly parallel to the coast. These were formed during the past two million years from wind-blown beach sand deposits along previous shorelines of this coastal plain.

The coastal woodlands are a distinctively different community to that of the forests of the range. Compare the rocks and gravels of the range with the sands of the plain; the tall trees of the forest with the shorter-trunked, deep-crowned woodland trees and shrublands on the plain.

The Wetlands of Lakes, Rivers, Streams and Estuaries

The apparent uniformity of the coastal woodlands is broken by urban developments and the wetlands of the coastal plain, which include the Swan and Canning Rivers and the chains of lakes to the north and south of the Swan.

The presence of wetlands is indicated by paperbark woodland, which is tolerant of wet conditions. The mostly smooth-barked and tall flooded gums, along with paperbarks, fringe watercourses and make walking alongside them an often pleasant and tranquil experience.

The many freshwater lakes, dotted throughout the coastal plain, appear like scattered jewels from vantage points through surrounding woodlands of banksia and paperbarks. These wetlands provide habitat for waders and other waterbirds.

The Coast and Marine Environments

The Perth Coast is a powerful line of demarcation between the coastal plain and the marine environment. Rocky limestone outcrops and sweeping white sand dunes with a plant cover of wattles and other shrubs, beautifully complement the blue-green waters of the Indian Ocean. Beneath the waves there is a seascape of limestone ledges, walls, caves, reefs and islands that provide habitat for a wonderful diversity of marine life.

WALKING SAFELY

There are basically two forms of walking in Perth Outdoors: strolling along an existing walktrail in a park, reserve, forest, bushland area or along the riverbank, or trekking through wild bush elsewhere. This book deals primarily with the first.

However, all natural areas have a degree of danger; for example, slippery or uneven surfaces. Walking along tracks, trails and firebreaks is relatively safe, but you should still be alert to potential hazards. Most of the information in this section is common sense, but additional safety and First Aid information have been included in the unlikely event of someone in your party being injured or getting lost.

Please take note of the following:

❖ Wear sturdy but comfortable shoes or boots. Training shoes may be suitable, but care should be taken when crossing uneven or slippery surfaces like mossy rocks. In these cases, it is desirable to wear boots that give some support to the ankles. Always wear good quality, fairly thick, cotton or wool socks.

❖ Long socks or long trousers, such as jeans or canvas drill, will give some leg protection against prickly vegetation or biting insects. A long-sleeved shirt will help protect you from sunburn in the summer and a woollen sweater or fleecy sweatshirt will help keep you warm in the winter. It is preferable to dress in layers of light clothing.

❖ Take a light raincoat.

❖ Wear a hat for protection against the sun or rain.

❖ Wear a sunscreen with a minimum sun protection factor (SPF) of 15+.

❖ Keep your things together in a light haversack or shoulder bag, to keep your hands free.

❖ If you are making an extended or difficult walk, tell at least two people and advise them when you've completed it.

❖ Take a first aid kit and insect repellent.

❖ Walk in a party of two or more people for safety. If you are injured, you will need someone who can summon help.

❖ Make sure you have adequate water: at least one litre per person on most days, and at least two litres on hot days.

❖ Take care not to trample sensitive areas such as moss-covered rock, sand dune plants or steep slopes.

If you become lost:

❖ Try to retrace your steps until you reach a recognisable place on the map.

❖ If you cannot retrace your steps, follow a track; it will usually lead to some habitation. Alternatively, head for the nearest high point and climb to the summit. You will then be able to see roads and areas of habitation.

❖ If you are still lost and you have run out of water, remember that animal trails always lead to water. Walk in the direction in which the trails converge into one. Watch out for flocks of birds; they fly rapidly towards water and more slowly when travelling away from water after drinking.

FIRST AID

Walking in the bush in Perth Outdoors is rarely dangerous. Nevertheless, walkers should be aware of possible hazards. The following section deals with the things you need to know in the unlikely event of one of your party being injured.

Your first aid kit should contain the following basic essentials:
Antiseptic cream and swabs
Aspirin or Paracetamol
Band Aids
Butterfly wound enclosures
Dressings (sterile)
Scissors
Snake bite bandage
Triangular bandage
Tweezers

Snake bites

Although several species of snake inhabit the areas dealt with in this book, it is very unlikely that you will see one, let alone be bitten by one. Snakes sense the vibration of approaching footsteps and tend to flee into the undergrowth. If you *are* unlucky enough to be bitten, here is what you should and should not do.

Assume the snake is poisonous and take the following action:

DO NOT panic: Try to remain calm, lie down and immobilise the bitten area.
DO NOT wash the wound: Venom left on the skin will help doctors identify the snake and administer the appropriate anti-venin.
DO NOT apply a tourniquet: Take out the snake bandage and bind, not too tightly, along the limb starting at the bite area, then bandage down the limb and continue back up above the bite area. This will help prevent the spread of the venom through the body. Do not remove the bandage.
DO NOT elevate the limb or attempt to walk or run: Movement will encourage the spread of the venom through the body. If necessary, immobilise the limb with a splint. Lie down and keep still until help arrives.
DO NOT attempt to catch the snake: Two bitten people will be more difficult to deal with than one, and if there are only two of you, you'll need someone who can go for help.

Sprains and Broken Limbs

Although most of the walks in this book are along existing, well-walked trails, some have uneven or loose surfaces along the route. Where possible, these have been indicated in the text, but you should always tread carefully as areas can become loose or uneven after heavy rain or very dry periods. If you or a fellow walker trips and sprains or breaks a limb, you should take the following action.

With sprains apply the 'RICE' technique:

R- REST and reassure the casualty.
I - ICE: Apply an ice pack, or cloth soaked in cold water, for 20 minutes. It may be reapplied every two hours for the first 24 hours.
C- COMPRESSION: Bandage the sprain firmly.
E- ELEVATE the sprained limb and support the injury.

Remember to avoid both heat and massage.

If the limb is broken and the casualty is conscious and breathing freely, take the following action:

DO control any bleeding.
DO rest and reassure the casualty.
DO immobilise the fractured limb with splints and slings in the most comfortable position and check the blood circulation past the last bandaging point. Be sure to handle the casualty carefully.
DO NOT pull on any fractures.
DO NOT give the casualty anything to drink.
DO NOT force or straighten fractured joints.

The First Aid information provided here is very basic. St John Ambulance Australia publishes First Aid manuals and runs a variety of First Aid courses. For more information contact your nearest St John Ambulance Centre.

WHAT YOU NEED TO KNOW

Bushwalking

You can bushwalk in two ways: by using walktrails or trekking through wild bush. While the first is usually safe and relaxing, the second can do environmental damage and put your life at risk.

The walks in this book follow either formalised walktrails with signs and occasionally surfaced tracks, or well used and informally established tracks through bushland, parks or riverside areas. Some of the walks cross or form part of the Bibbulmun Track. This is a 650 kilometre long-distance walk track from Kalamunda, in the Darling Range east of Perth, to Walpole, on the south coast.

Camping

While out walking you may see possible sites for a future camping expedition.

As more and more people head for the bush, greater pressures are put on our natural resources. In an effort to protect our environment, visitors may only camp at designated camping sites - usually marked with a sign in national parks, regional parks, State forest or bush areas. Please leave no rubbish or other traces of your visit.

Camping fees are charged in some areas and the funds raised help to pay for the facilities and services provided.

Dieback

Some areas of forest and woodland have been infected by a soil-borne fungus (*Phytophthora cinnamomi*) that attacks the root systems of trees, shrubs and wildflowers. The disease is known to attack at least 900 plant species and many, such as banksias and dryandras, die very quickly. The fungus travels over and through the soil in water, attaching spores to roots. The rot sets in immediately.

The fungus is carried in soil or mud that sticks to boots and shoes, and the wheels, mudguards and underbodies of vehicles. When the soil or mud drops off, the fungus immediately contaminates the new area and multiplies. There is, as yet, no known cure.

Some areas in national parks and State forest are closed to vehicles to prevent dieback being carried into or spread through them. These areas are largely uninfected. You may enter on foot but you must not take vehicles, motorbikes, horses or any form of wheeled transport into these areas. When walking through infected areas, help stop the rot by not straying from the track. Observe the signs and give our plants a chance.

Entry Fees ($)

Entry fees are charged to some national parks, regional parks and reserves. Where a charge is made, it is indicated in this book by the symbol ($). The funds raised help to pay for the facilities and services provided.

Fire

Fire is a good servant but a poor master. Bushfires are a real danger, particularly during the dry summer months.

Please note these points:

- ❖ Always use the fireplaces provided. Better still, bring your own portable stove.
- ❖ Open fires are not permitted in national parks.
- ❖ Build a stone ring in State forest if no fireplace exists, or dig a shallow pit to contain the embers.
- ❖ Clear all leaf litter, dead branches and anything else that may burn from an area of at least three metres around and above the fire. This also applies to portable stoves.
- ❖ Never leave a fire unattended.
- ❖ Make sure the fire is completely out before leaving. Use soil and water to extinguish the embers, and bury the ashes.

On certain days during the year the fire forecast is 'very high' or 'extreme'. A total fire ban exists on these days. Local radio stations broadcast fire risk warnings, but please check with Shire authorities, the tourist bureau, or the nearest CALM office for advice on the fire situation.

Firearms

No offensive weapon is to be brought into any conservation or recreation area.

Fishing

Fisheries regulations apply in all areas, but you should also check with the ranger in any national park. Trout and redfin perch have been stocked in inland waters near Perth. Marron fishing is a seasonal activity by permit only. We'd like you to come back, so help conserve fish numbers by taking only enough for your immediate needs.

Granite outcrops

Several walks in this book cross or pass close to granite outcrops. Granite outcrops, often termed 'living rocks', are unique sanctuaries for many species of plants and animals. Exploring granite outcrops is a fascinating experience, but the environment is extremely fragile. Moving a rock, disturbing a plant or carelessly placing a foot can cause irreparable damage. Please do not stray off the tracks that cross granite outcrops.

Native plants and animals

In order to protect the environment, please do not disturb any native animals, and do not pick the wildflowers. Rocks, vegetation or old logs should not be removed as these are often the homes of small creatures that depend on such habitats for existence.

Pets

Pets are not permitted in national parks, nature reserves and water catchments. Many other shire-controlled parks and reserves have similar restrictions. If you are not sure whether dogs and/or other pets are permitted at the place you intend to visit, please leave them at home.

Rubbish

Place all litter in bins provided. If there are no bins, take your litter home with you. When camping or walking in the bush, bury organic waste at least 15 centimetres deep and at least 100 metres from any waterway, picnic area or campsite.

Vehicles

Normal road rules apply in all recreation and conservation areas. To protect wildlife habitat and the environment from erosion and dieback disease, please keep to formed roads and designated tracks at all times. Be sure to lock your vehicle if it is left unattended.

Water

Most creeks and rivers in Western Australia are dry during summer months. When you are out and about take your own drinking water. If you do have to use water from the few permanent water points, it should be boiled before use, or purified using a commercially available purification product.

Water Catchments

These special areas are reserved for water and vegetation protection. Because of this, there are restrictions on various recreation activities in certain areas. Check with the WA Water Authority.

Remember

❖ **Be careful:** Stay on paths and help prevent erosion. Your safety in natural areas is our concern, but your responsibility.
❖ **Be clean:** Take your rubbish out with you. Don't use soap or detergent in rivers or streams; they kill the aquatic life.
❖ **Be cool:** Light fires only in fireplaces. Bring your own portable gas stove. Take notice of all fire weather forecasts.
❖ **Protect animals and plants:** No firearms, please. Pets are not permitted in national parks and in some other areas. Check before you bring your dog or cat.
❖ **Stay on the road:** Follow signs and stay on the roads designated. Normal road rules apply.

YANCHEP NATIONAL PARK.

The Hills   Walks 1 - 13

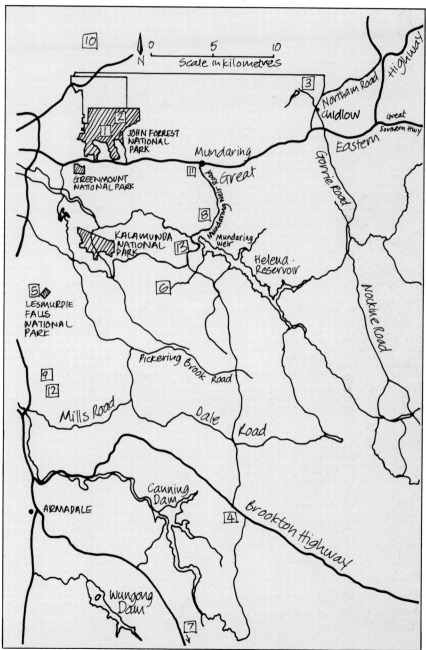

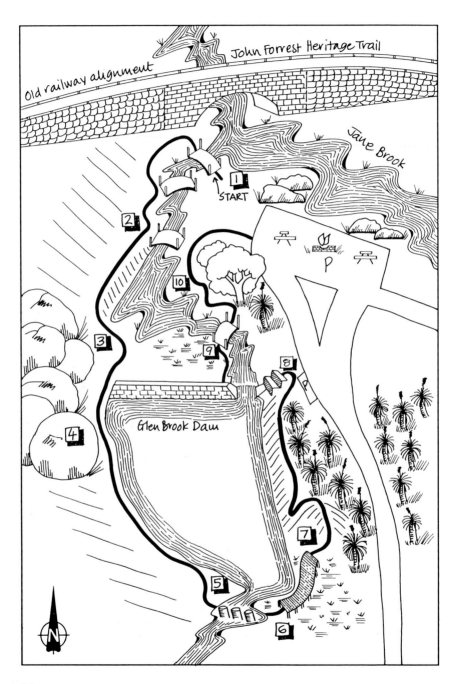

Old railway alignment

John Forrest Heritage Trail

Jane Brook

START

Glen Brook Dam

N

Glen Brook Trail

John Forrest National Park ($)

Length: *2.2 kilometres loop*
Grade: *2*
Walk time: *45 minutes*

This walk starts and finishes at the main picnic area in John Forrest National Park and skirts the Glen Brook Dam. It features scenic views over the dam and a multitude of wildflowers during spring.

1   Leave from the north-west corner of the picnic area and cross a footbridge over Glen Brook where it converges with Jane Brook. Turn left after crossing the bridge and head along the brook side.
2   An old 1930s-style picnic shelter, nestled below the steep hillside covered in wandoo-marri-jarrah woodland, overlooks the current picnic area on the opposite side of the brook. Small bridges cross the brook. From here, the track rises slowly towards the dam.
3   The Glen Brook Dam was built in the 1960s to provide additional water supplies for the park. Follow the trail around the dam.
4   A large granite outcrop on the right of the trail is set back among the trees on the slope.
5   Cross over Glen Brook at the southern end of the dam using stepping posts. The brook flows only in winter.
6   Head north again on the boardwalk over a swampy area.
7   The trail climbs over a small ridge from which there are elevated views of the dam. Blackboys dominate the slopes on this side.
8   On reaching the dam wall, step down onto the wall and cross the spillway.
9   Descend more steps and rejoin the trail below. Cross the footbridge over the spillway.
10 The trail follows the line of the brook back to the picnic area.

David Briggs

Where is it?: *26 km east of Perth in John Forrest National Park.*
Travelling time: *40 minutes from Perth via Great Eastern Highway.*
Facilities: *BBQs, kiosk, tavern, tables, water, toilets, carpark.*
On-site information: *Trailhead sign, directional signs along the route.*
Best season: *All year, spring for wildflowers.*

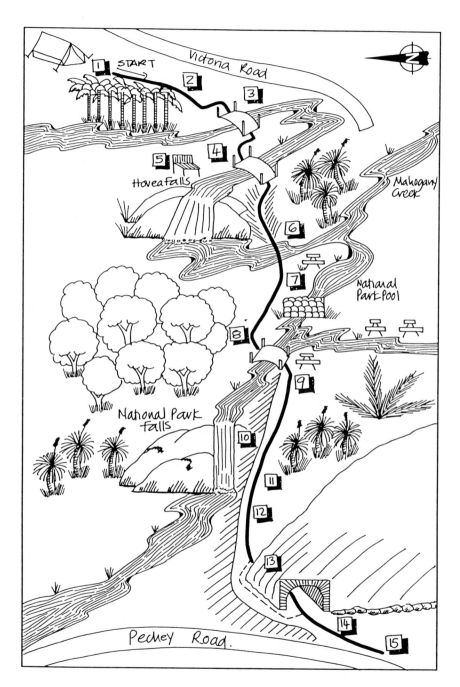

John Forrest Heritage Trail **2**

John Forrest National Park ($)

Length: 10.2 kilometres return
Grade: 3
Walk time: 2 hours 15 minutes

This walk runs along the route of the old Eastern Railway line, which passed through the National Park. It is a long, sloping walk from east to west with ballast under foot. The walk can be taken from either Pechey Road or Victoria Road end, or part-way from the main picnic area near the old National Park Station.

1   Hovea Station campsite.
2   Hovea Station was the first siding where visitors could alight from the train. A crossing loop was constructed in 1912 as a place for loading timber. Eight large palms mark the site of the station.
3   About 600 metres from Hovea Station is a pair of old railway bridges for two-way traffic.
4   A second pair of bridges is a further 200 metres along the trail.
5   Hovea Falls is named after the holly-leafed hovea, which, when in season, can be seen in the vicinity.
6   Deep Creek Bridge. Although now filled beneath, the original bridge remains and you can still see the timbers. At 125.7 metres, this was the longest trestle bridge constructed on this line.
7   The main picnic area is adjacent to the Jane Brook, below the walkway. The steps, garden walls and footpaths were constructed by sustenance workers during the Great Depression of the 1930s.
8   Jane Brook Bridge was built on this site in 1895. In the 1920s it deteriorated such that gravel was used for reinforcement. In 1928 the structure was changed to steel and concrete to cater for heavier loads.
9   The foundations seen here are all that remains of National Park Station, which was built for park visitors in 1936 as an alternative stop to Hovea Station.
10   National Park Falls. Jane Brook drops some 25 metres over massive granite rocks, which outcrop from the ancient bedrock of the Darling Scarp. The falls are at their best during and after winter rains between July and September.
11   On 30 June 1896, a goods and passenger train bound for Northam set down passengers at Lion Mill, 13.5 kilometres up the line from here. A coupling broke soon afterwards and 22 of its 24 carriages started rolling towards Perth. They crashed here at 193 kph, killing eight horses and one person.

12 At this point there are excellent views across the valley to the Swan Coastal Plain.
13 Old Railway Tunnel. This tunnel, completed in 1895, is 240 metres in length and is the only main railway tunnel in WA. You may walk through the tunnel or skirt around the outside.
14 This is the site of the main campsite that housed the railway construction team in tents.
15 The end of the walk at Pechey Road. Arrange to be collected here or return along the same route to Victoria Road.

Karl Mucjanko and Mark Moore

Where is it?: *26 km east of Perth in John Forrest National Park. The trail starts from Victoria Road, Hovea.*

Travelling time: *40 minutes from Perth via Great Eastern Highway and Brooking Road.*

Facilities: *BBQs, kiosk, tavern, tables, water, toilets, carpark in Park.*

On-site information: *Trailhead signs (both ends), interpretation plaques along the route.*

Best season: *Autumn, winter for falls, spring for wildflowers.*

BLACKBOYS

One of the commonest plants in our local bush is the blackboy (or grasstree).

Around Perth, five different species occur; some have no trunk, some a very spiky flower and another has comparatively small clumps of foliage and a slender flower spike.

Grasstrees only grow in Australia and there are 28 species altogether, nine of which occur in Western Australia. They were a tremendous resource for Aboriginal people. Food, materials for building shelters and tools for fire lighting are only some of the many uses of this plant.

Possibly the most well-known and easily recognised species in the Perth Outdoors area is *Xanthorrhoea preissii*, known as 'Balga' by the local Nyoongar people. This species develops a tall, sometimes twisted trunk and is the only one to grow above three metres in height.

The *Xanthorrhoea preissii* grows an impressive spear or flower spike up to four metres in length and six centimetres thick. Thousands of buds are tightly packed on the top two thirds of the spear and open into white flowers in mid to late spring. After flowering, the spear produces beak-like capsules, which release shiny black seeds in summer and autumn.

Grasstrees are found in the western parts of the South West, from north of Geraldton to Esperance, on the south coast, where they grow on a wide range of soils. One species occurs in the desert.

GRASS TREE

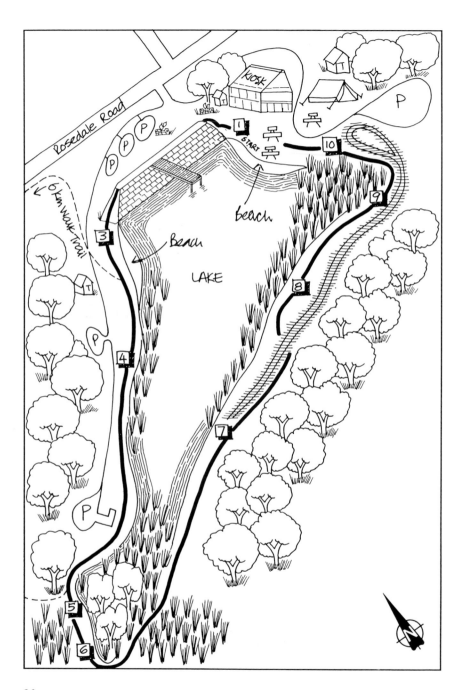

Lakeside Walktrail **3**

Lake Leschenaultia ($)

Length: *3 kilometres loop*
Grade: *2*
Walk time: *1 hour*

This is a very pleasant walk around the lake, especially after a barbecue lunch. For the more adventurous, there is a longer walk that takes you through the jarrah forest to the west of the lake.

Note: Dogs are not permitted in the park.

1 Start at the east end of the dam wall adjacent to the main picnic area.
2 Midway along the wall is a diving platform. Swimming in the lake is a popular summer pastime. Leave the dam wall and turn left and follow the track along the beach front.
3 The six kilometre walktrail branches off at this point.
4 This section is dominated by jarrah-marri woodlands on the slopes to the right and reeds around the lake's edge.
5 The reeds become more prominent at the south-west corner of the lake. Here, the longer trail rejoins.
6 As you turn at the far end of the lake, paperbarks are found in wet areas on each side of the track.
7 Heading back up along the eastern side of the lake you come to the terminus of the miniature railway.
8 Wandoos dominate the vegetation beyond the railway track.
9 At the east corner of the lake there are more reeds and orange wattle (*Acacia salignia*).
10 Continue past the railway station and across lawns to the main picnic area.

Alan Hill

Where is it?: *40 km east of Perth, north of Chidlow.*
Travelling time: *1 hour from Perth via Great Eastern Highway.*
Facilities: *BBQs, picnic sites, water, toilets, carparks, kiosk.*
On-site information: *Occasional trail markers.*
Best season: *All year.*

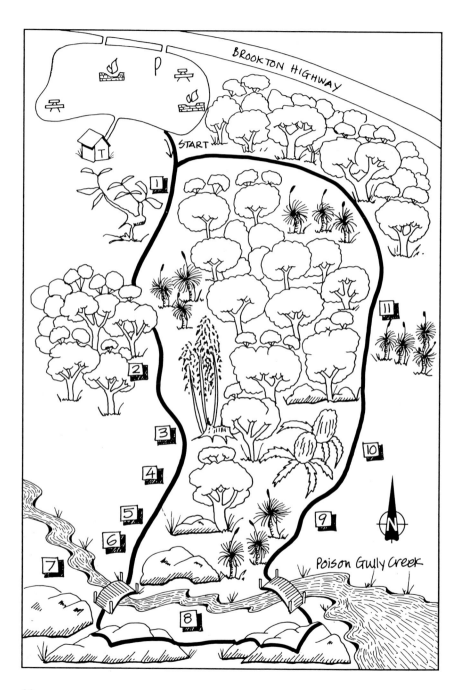

Lesley Nature Trail 4

Length: *1.5 kilometres loop*
Grade: *2*
Walk time: *45 minutes*

A forest is a complex biological community of living organisms that is continually changing. This trail takes you through the forest life cycle and features forestry techniques and tree species of the northern jarrah forest. Points of interest along the route are marked by numbered pegs.

1   Looking closely at seedlings on the ground you may see a woody lump or lignotuber. In its first year, jarrah (*Eucalyptus marginata*) produces a small lignotuber at the base of its stem. This is an organ of food storage and regeneration, and contains a store of living buds. Small shoots will emerge and as the lignotuber becomes larger, the plant will produce a single vigorous stem, which eventually becomes the trunk of a new tree.

2   Once the single shoot has emerged, the young jarrah tree will continue to grow into a pole, unless damaged by insect attack, fire or frost. Jarrah is characterised by grey stringy bark and a straight trunk, which can reach a height of 20 metres and two metres diameter.

3   Many eucalypts, including jarrah, may regenerate by coppice shoots from a stump. These form when a mature tree is damaged by wind or storm, or when it is cut down.

4   Not all trees, even those of the same species, develop into a form that will be useful for timber. Some may develop large, heavy limbs and crooked trunks, while others may have been damaged by intense wildfire or insect attack.

5   Some trees are removed to make way for young regrowth. Others are retained as food and shelter for wildlife, and to stabilise the soil. An old method used to kill a tree was ringbarking. A strip of the outer living wood of the trunk (which transports water and nutrients) was removed and the tree eventually died.

6   Another common tree of the jarrah forest is marri (*Eucalyptus calophylla*). This tree is easily recognised by its large gumnuts and the red gum seen oozing from its trunk. This is caused by insects boring into the heartwood and releasing the characteristic red sap.

7   The trail crosses a small stream known as Poison Gully. A shrub called York Road poison (*Gastrolobium calycinum*) grows in this valley and is toxic all year round, hence the gully's name.

8 As the trail meanders along the stream you will see a decline in the number of trees, while the scrub becomes thicker. Here the soil may be very shallow or non-existent, and large areas of exposed rock appear. Although trees find it difficult to survive in this environment, other plants, such as blackboys (*Xanthorrhoea preissii*), have adapted and thrive. Thicker creek vegetation is a particularly good habitat for most South West fauna.

9 Apart from jarrah and marri, several other tree species are found in the Perth Outdoors area. Yarri (*Eucalyptus patens*), also called blackbutt, grows in moist areas along creeks and rivers. Although similar to jarrah, yarri can be recognised by its drooping blue-green leaves, which are longer and narrower than those of jarrah, and the fibrous, deeply fissured bark of mature trees. Along the trail you will walk through a buttress of large yarris.

10 Another tree found in the understorey of the jarrah forest is the bull banksia (*Banksia grandis*), distinguishable by its large serrated leaves. Its yellow, candle-shaped flowers, large woody cone and gnarled growth habit make it an attractive forest species. It is one of several plants that are very susceptible to dieback, caused by the soil-borne fungus *Phytophthora cinnamoni*.

11 This tree was left during the 1950 logging operation to provide a seed source for regeneration. The small trees you can see surrounding this large one are the results of this modern management technique, which ensures that for every jarrah tree removed there will be at least one young seedling ready to take its place.

Peter Gibson

Where is it?: *47 km from Perth and about 20 km east of Kelmscott along Brookton Highway.*
Travelling time: *1 hour.*
Facilities: *BBQs, toilets, carpark.*
On-site information: *Marker pegs along trail.*
Best season: *Spring for wildflowers.*

BRUSHTAIL POSSUM

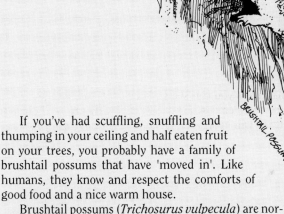

If you've had scuffling, snuffling and thumping in your ceiling and half eaten fruit on your trees, you probably have a family of brushtail possums that have 'moved in'. Like humans, they know and respect the comforts of good food and a nice warm house.

Brushtail possums (*Trichosurus vulpecula*) are normally found in open forests and woodland where they nest high up in tree hollows, although they spend considerable amounts of time on the ground. Often they occupy the same tree for years, or even generations.

Male brushtail possums are territorial. Females seem to be more flexible and will occasionally share territories with other females, or move in and share a male's home tree when nesting.

After the young are born and weaned, they move out to seek their own trees and territories some distance from their mother's home range.

The main requirement of any brushtail possum is a suitably sized hollow high enough above the ground. Because large cavities in trees are usually formed by broken branches, possum trees tend to be large, old, in decline or dead. You can usually tell a possum tree by the pathway of scratch marks that leads up the trunk and, sometimes, droppings at the base of the tree.

Brushtail possums are nocturnal so you will be lucky to see one during the day.

Lesmurdie Falls Walktrail   5

Lesmurdie Falls National Park

Length: *2 kilometres return*
Grade: *4*
Walk time: *1 hour 30 minutes*

The main feature of this walk is the falls and there is a viewing platform that provides views both up and down the valley. For the most part, the trail runs gradually downhill on the side of the valley, before descending more steeply to the edge of the brook near the end. Allow ample time to return along the track, which climbs constantly until you reach the top of the falls. There are several bird species in the area, including kestrels, and the sounds of frogs can be heard after winter rains. This walk is particularly rewarding in early spring when the park is ablaze with wildflowers and the brook is still flowing strongly over the falls.

1 Walking down from the western end of the carpark you pass through a pleasant picnic area with barbecues and ample tables. The trail continues down a slight slope.
2 When you reach the small bridge over the brook, do not cross, but turn left along the blue metal track by the side of the brook. This part of the trail features marris, rushes and sedges by the water's edge and granite outcrops on your left. Another track joins from the left and a second bridge crosses the brook.
3 As you rise up you will get your first views out over the city and coastal plain.
4 Descending slightly you come to an old concrete bridge over the top of the falls. The bridge is now closed but you can still see over the falls from here.
5 A little further on, down some steps, you come to an observation platform. From here, there are extensive views of the city, with its perpendicular tower block thrusting from the surrounding coastal plain. Looking back you can see the upper falls and the heathland across the valley.
6 Continue the slow descent along the side of the valley. Uphill of the trail you will see granite outcrops and a heath of blackboys, wattles, grevilleas and a multitude of other flowering plants. Downhill are wandoos on the slopes and marris by the brook. As the trail winds between a cluster of granite rocks, you will see several zamias. Look back to see the entire falls.
7 Cross a small wooden bridge that runs over a floodway. On the opposite side of the valley is a firebreak or track that winds up the hillside. Continue your descent until it turns right and heads downhill.
8 This part of the trail is fairly steep and may be uneven underfoot, so care should

be taken. The trail winds to the side of the brook, meeting another track that runs along the water's edge. Turn left and follow the track.

9   This section is typical riverside vegetation: marris, sedges and grasses. Opposite are wandoos on the rising slope. There are also coral vines (*Kennedia coccinea*) and the rare Helena velvet bush (*Lasiopetalum bracteatum*). Western king parrots can sometimes be seen in the branches of the marris.

10 Kalamunda Shire carpark. Return along the same route to the falls picnic area or arrange for someone to collect you.

David Briggs and Keith Tresidder

Where is it?: *22 km east of Perth on Falls Road, Lesmurdie.*
Travelling time: *30 minutes from Perth.*
Facilities: *BBQs, tables, water, toilets, carpark.*
On-site information: *Information shelter in picnic area, arrows along trail.*
Best season: *Winter for falls, spring for falls and wildflowers.*

AUSTRALIAN KESTREL

The Australian kestrel (*Falco cenchroides*) is usually seen singly as it sits quietly on power poles or the very tips of tall trees observing all around in search of insects, lizards and small rodents.

These handsome, but small, birds of prey are about 32 centimetres long, with tail, back and wings of a bright rufous brown, marked with black. The underparts are creamy white to the knees of yellow legs.

Kestrels are a common sight along the open grass country along the coast and many pairs nest in niches in limestone cliffs either on the mainland or on offshore islands. Inland the birds lay their eggs in tree hollows, on buildings or on cliff faces.

They are often observed head to wind, hovering while the head is down turned, looking for prey. When it spies its prey, the bird drops like a stone to impale its chosen morsel on razor sharp talons, then alights with it to a favoured pole or fence post, where a strong curved beak dismembers the food.

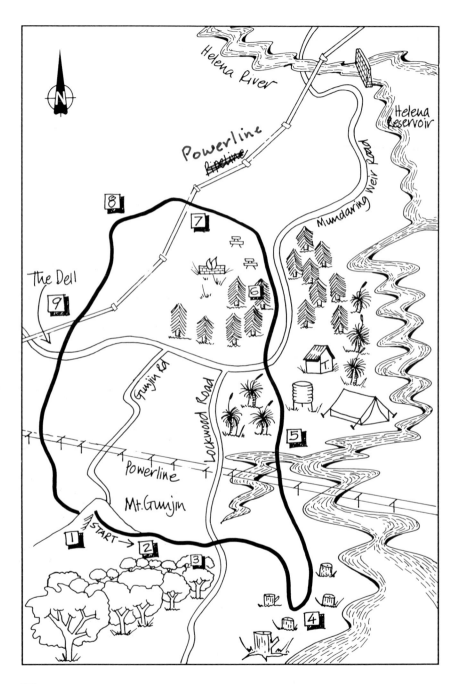

Little Oven Circuit   6

Length: *12 kilometres loop*
Grade: *4*
Walk time: *4 hours*

This is a detour circuit off the Bibbulmun Track. The first part of the walk follows along the Bibbulmun Track before diverting to the Little Oven Campsite, Farrell Grove and The Dell. Good views can be had from various points along the walk.

1   Mt Gunjin is 398 metres high and was the site of a single-pole fire lookout tower - one of a series running from the south coast to north of Perth. The tower was demolished in the late 1980s because it was considered unsafe and too costly to maintain.
2   The trail wanders down a gentle slope through jarrah regrowth forest. Sunlight filters through a dense understorey of blackboy, bull banksia and sheoaks. Purple-coloured hoveas, and native grasses such as purple flag and the yellow-flowered *Patersonia umbrosa* form. *xanthina*, line the walk.
3   At the turn of the century this forest was heavily cut over and ringbarked to provide Perth residents with timber and fuel, and to increase the runoff into the Helena River reservoir.
4   Here, the track turns left (north) and leaves the Bibbulmun Track, heading towards the campsite. There is plentiful birdlife among the dryandras, and numerous old tree stumps are visible from the track.
5   Crossing a small creek, lined with blackbutts, you will come across the campsite nestled in the hillside beneath marri and jarrah trees. The tent sites are set among a dense stand of blackboys and banksias on a gentle slope. Facilities include a toilet and rainwater tank.
6   The track crosses Mundaring Weir Road and passes through mature piastre pines towards Farrell Grove recreation site, which has BBQs, picnic tables, toilets, play equipment and plenty of open space, and then follows the Winjan Track for a short distance.
7   Passing beneath the powerlines, you are given partial views across the valley of Mundaring Weir and the Devenish pine plantation. The track joins the Kattamorda Heritage Trail.
8   This part of the walk follows the route of an old tramway line built in 1908 and used to transport timber from the Post and Honey sawmill, at The Dell, to Mundaring Weir.

9   The Dell recreation site with BBQs, picnic tables and toilets. From here the track continues along an abandoned tramway, crossing Mundaring Weir Road and climbing uphill to Mt Gungin, the starting point.

Jamie Ridley

Where is it?: *40 km from Perth. Access to Mt Gungin is from Mundaring Weir Road via Gungin Road.*
Travelling time: *1 hour from Perth.*
Facilities: *Fire ring and picnic table at trailhead. More extensive facilities at sites* en route.
On-site information: *Bibbulmun Track signs (red Waugal) at the start and along the walk, as well as interpretive signs.*
Best season: *Spring for wildflowers, autumn for running water in creeks.*

CHUDITCH

The chuditch (*Dasyurus geoffroii*) is one of four species of so-called native cats or quolls found in Australia and is Western Australia's largest marsupial predator. It has brown fur with white spots and moves very quickly on the ground, climbs efficiently and may dig or occupy existing holes in the ground. Activity is at its greatest around dawn and dusk.

The term 'cat' is a misnomer as the chuditch is a marsupial and therefore more closely related to kangaroos and possums. More commonly used is the local Aboriginal name 'chuditch', which mimics the guttural call the animal makes when it is disturbed.

Being a most aggressive carnivore, the chuditch feeds on a wide variety of small mammals, birds, insects and carrion. Since the arrival of Europeans to this land, poultry runs and rubbish bins have been raided with relish.

The young are carried in a pouch for approximately 11 weeks. By about mid-September they are deposited in a safe den (hollow log or burrow) and can continue to be fed by their mother until they leave the den and disperse around December to January.

Although breeding programs have seen the release of animals back into the wild at Julimar Forest Park and trapping has indicated that there are populations in many parts of the south-western corner of WA, the chuditch is still one of our most threatened species.

Mt Cooke Walktrail

Length: *7 kilometres return*
Grade: *5*
Walk time: *2 hours 30 minutes*

Mt Cooke is the highest point in the Darling Range, being 582 metres above sea level. During the ascent you pass through areas of jarrah forest, much of which has been quarantined from dieback since the mid 1970s. On the south-western slopes are stands of Darling Range ghost gum (*Eucalyptus laelia*), an uncommon eucalypt on the eastern extremity of its range. The walk features a variety of plant species, scenic views and spectacular granite outcrops.

1 From the carpark, walk up a steep slope to a granite outcrop. From here there are good views over the Cooke Plantation to the south-east.
2 At the end of the outcrop are stands of wandoo and Darling Range ghost gum. This part of the track is very slippery when wet and you should be very careful.
3 The track passes through an outcrop of large rounded boulders with blackboys, hakeas and acacias. Further up are more boulders surrounded by forest.
4 The summit of the first peak provides good views back along the track.
5 Moving down into a picturesque saddle there are thick stands of ghost gum. Head for the large granite outcrop opposite and climb to the top.
6 Halfway to the summit of the second peak, look to the south-west and you will see the Del Park mine site on the horizon.
7 The summit of the second peak. A steel survey peg has been driven into the rock and from here you get good views of Mt Cooke to the north.
8 Cross the saddle towards the base of Mt Cooke. From here the track zig-zags to the summit.
9 The summit provides excellent views across the range and over the coastal plain to the ocean. Return to the start along the same route.

Ken Wheeler and Grant Hansen

Where is it?: *72 km south-east of Perth on Albany Highway.*
Travelling time: *1 hour 40 minutes from Perth.*
Facilities: *Carpark in old picnic area adjacent to Cooke Plantation.*
On-site information: *None.*
Best season: *Autumn, winter, spring for wildflowers.*

Kalgoorlie Pipeline

Mundaring Weir Road

Fred Jacoby Park

START

N

Portagabra Track   **8**

Fred Jacoby Park

Length: *3.8 kilometres loop*
Grade: *5*
Walk time: *2 hours*

A challenging walk featuring granite outcrops, wandoo woodlands and views of Mt Dale to the south-east.

1 The trail begins at the north-east end of Fred Jacoby Park. The area was settled in the 1830s by James Drummond, the Swan River Colony's first botanist. In 1889, the 1124 hectare property was sold to the Jacobys, who named it Portagabra. In 1954, the property was given to the people of WA as a recreation area.

2 The track passes beneath the 557 kilometre pipeline that supplies water to the Goldfields. Work on the pipeline began in 1898 and was completed in 1903.

3 At this point you can see the remains of an old fenceline on the Portagabra property.

4 After crossing a creek, which flows in winter and early spring, the track narrows and slowly winds along the creek edge.

5 As you meander up a steady rise the creek is lined with granite outcrops and open wandoo woodland.

6 The track turns to cross the creek at a small soak (wet area) lined with tea tree.

7 From here the track becomes steeper and moves through jarrah and marri woodland with blackboy understorey. Numerous large stumps scattered through the area are evidence of logging activities around the turn of the century.

8 As the track climbs to the upper slopes of the ridge through a spectacular granite outcrop, the forest to the south-east comes into view. This part of the track is quite steep with several steps. The top of the slope is a good resting spot.

9 The narrow track comes out onto an old track running across the ridge. From here you can see Mt Dale to the south-east. A short distance along, the track begins to descend steeply and gives spectacular panoramic views.

10 Near the bottom of the slope is a large hollow tree by the side of the track. It offers shelter to three or four people during rain.

11 A log bench, set beneath the spreading crown of a snottygobble (*Persoonia elliptica*), makes an ideal resting place with views along the creek line.

12 This dense grove of parrotbush (*Dryandra sessilis*) is a favourite habitat for a

variety of birds including splendid wrens, honeyeaters, scarlet robins, and larger birds like magpies and twenty-eight parrots.

13 The track continues downwards through the Devenish Plantation, a plantation of *Pinus radiata* established in 1958 and named after Fred Jacoby's daughter Mrs Elfreda Devenish. From here you cross over the pipeline to return to the park.

Jamie Ridley

Where is it?: *Fred Jacoby Park, 37 km from Perth on Mundaring Weir Road.*
Travelling time: *45 minutes from Perth.*
Facilities: *BBQs, playground, toilets, disabled toilets, carpark.*
On-site information: *Trailhead sign, directional signs along route.*
Best season: *Late winter and spring for wildflowers and running water.*

MOSSES, LIVERWORTS, LICHENS AND FUNGI

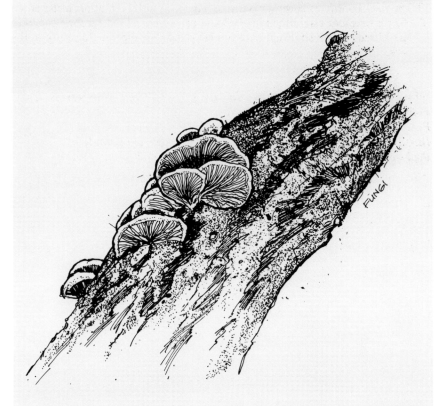

FUNGI

What we normally see around us are the vascular plants, that is, the ferns and flowering plants. There are also non-vascular plants that, because of their size and unusual habitat, usually go unnoticed.

These plants consist of the Bryophites (mosses and liverworts) and the Thallophytes (algae, fungi and lichens).

Mosses, liverworts and lichens frequently form diverse communities on granite rocks throughout the south-west of Western Australia.

The mosses and liverworts have a simple form, small size and are quite unrelated to all other general plant life. Lichens are of particular interest because they are composed of alga (green or blue green) and a fungus.

Macro-fungi (mushrooms, toadstools and puffballs) are usually found on decaying wood, in damp soil and among forest floor leaf litter. In winter, they show a spectacular array of fruiting bodies of all shapes, sizes and colours.

Sixty-foot Falls Walk

Ellis Brook

Length: 2 *kilometres loop*
Grade: 3
Walk time: 1 *hour*

This is the shorter of two walktrails and takes in the falls. It has some steep sections where the ground may be unstable underfoot and walkers should take special care. The falls and wildflowers in spring are undoubtedly the main features of the walk, as is the exposed granite rock of the area, particularly where the brook tumbles over the falls. The area is rich in plant life and more than 100 different species may easily be observed along the walk.

1 Start from the south-east corner of the carpark and proceed along a boardwalk towards granite outcrops.
2 Along the stream banks is dense closed scrub and colourful heath where the granite outcrops occur. The vegetation on the north and south-facing slopes of the valley is noticeably different because of the differing amounts of sunlight each receives.
3 Close to the small steps, the brook cascades over small rocky shelves.
4 Here, there are excellent views of the falls.
5 From the top of the waterfall there are superb views down the valley to Perth. A very large granite outcrop marks an ideal picnic spot. In an area above the falls there is a stand of rare salmon white gum.
6 From here there are views into the deep quarry, which was once a source of road-making material, but is now a favourite spot of rock climbers and abseilers.
7 A smaller quarry is on the left of the track.
8 The track follows the quarry access road for a short distance before heading down a flight of steps to cross the brook and finish back in the carpark.

Angela Stuart-Street

Where is it?: 25 *km south of Perth, access is from Rushton Road.*
Travelling time: 45 *minutes from Perth.*
Facilities: Carpark, picnic spot above the falls.
On-site information: Trail markers in places along route.
Best season: All year, spring for wildflowers.

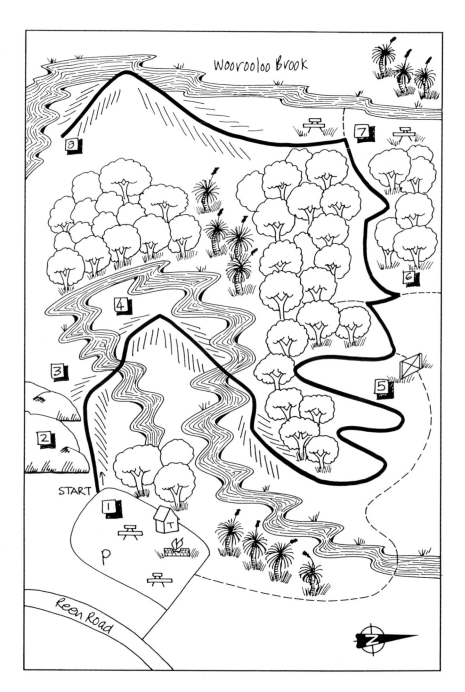

Woorooloo Brook

Slippery Dip Walktrail

10

F R Berry Reserve

Length: *3.5 kilometres return*
Grade: *2*
Walk time: *1 hour 30 minutes*

This walk winds through the reserve to Woorooloo Brook, where there is a picnic spot and a water slide called the 'Slippery Dip'. There are spectacular views to be had from various parts of the trail and during spring the wildflowers are abundant.

1   Starting from the east side of the picnic area, the trail heads east.
2   Soon after the start there are large granite outcrops on the left.
3   Another walktrail branches off to the left. Continue ahead.
4   The trail turns northwards and crosses a winter creek twice before winding along the edge of woodland.
5   On the right of the track is a gate through which another track passes and returns to the carpark. This is an option you may wish to take on your return from the Slippery Dip.
6   Another track crosses the trail here. Continue ahead through a grove of trees towards Woorooloo Brook.
7   Here the woodland opens up and the trail emerges at a pleasant picnic area by the side of the brook. Turn left and follow the brook to the Slippery Dip. On the opposite side of the brook, the ground rises steeply and the hillside is a mass of wildflowers during spring.
8   The Slippery Dip is spectacular in winter and spring and is a popular summer attraction.
    Swimmers should exercise extreme care at the Slippery Dip. It is very deep and particularly hazardous after winter rains, when waters are fast flowing.

Denise Hamilton

Where is it?: *45 km north-east of Perth, near Gidgegannup. Access from Reen Road.*
Travelling time: *1 hour 15 minutes from Perth via Toodyay Road.*
Facilities: *Wood BBQs, toilets, carpark.*
On-site information: *Trailhead sign.*
Best season: *Spring for wildflowers, summer to enjoy the water.*

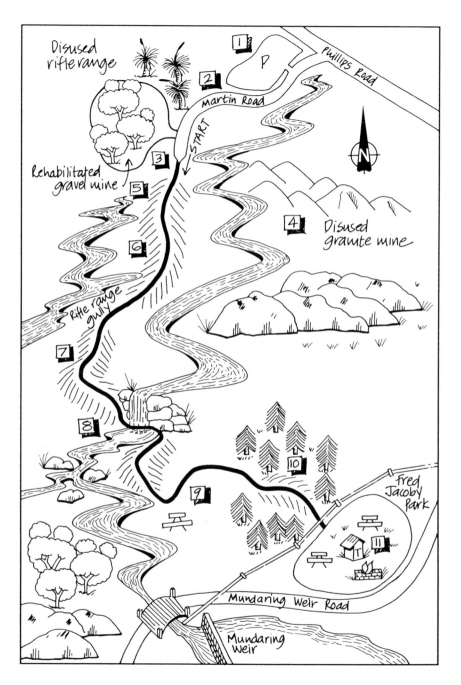

Southell Track

11

Length: *8.5 kilometres one-way*
Grade: *4*
Walk time: *3 hours*

This one-way walk, running from Martin Road in Mundaring to Fred Jacoby Park on Mundaring Weir Road, is a gentle descent for most of the way and provides great views of the Helena Valley. Birds and wildflowers are abundant at different times of the year and, if you look closely, you may see evidence (diggings and scats) of nocturnal animals such as bandicoots, brushtail possums and chuditch. You should arrange to be dropped off at the starting point and collected at the park.

1   The walk starts near a disused rifle range a few hundred metres right of the trailhead sign on Martin Road. The range is still visible through the regrowth.
2   Following Martin Road south you pass open marri and jarrah woodlands with a dense understorey of blackboys. During spring there is a magnificent display of wildflowers including kangaroo paws, donkey and spider orchids, prickly Moses, and hoveas.
3   Gravel Mine site, rehabilitated by local school children as an Arbor Day activity. Queensland silver wattles occur on both sides of the track and have yellow flowers in autumn and winter.
4   A disused granite mine is visible just over the creek 400 metres on the left, in private property.
5   The track moves through an area of parrot bushes, which have light yellow flowers in winter and attract a variety of birds. Blue wrens, rosellas and twenty-eight parrots can often be seen flitting from stem to stem.
6   As the track descends through banksia woodland, the south face of the Helena Valley appears at the end of Rifle Range Gully. Granite rock outcrops and the pale trunks of wandoos are clearly visible.
7   As the descent becomes a little steeper, you move through a grove of common sheoak (*Allocasuarina fraseriana*).
8   Continuing towards North Ledge, you come across Burke's Gully Waterfall, which cascades over granite rock through wandoo woodland and down towards the Helena River. Darwinias are visible on either side of the track near to where it joins the Lower Helena Bridle Trail for a short distance.
9   The track climbs steeply out of Burke's Gully along the upper edge of the valley, giving magnificent views of wandoo and granite outcrops along the breakaway

51

and into the valley. On arriving at North Ledge there is a picturesque view of Mundaring Weir, the O'Connor Museum and up the valley to the south-east.

10 The track descends and passes through the Devenish Plantation, named after Mrs Elfreda Devenish, daughter of Fred Jacoby.

11 Fred Jacoby Park.

Jamie Ridley

Where is it?: *30 km from Perth at Martin Road, Mundaring (signposted).*
Travelling time: *40 minutes from Perth.*
Facilities: *Carpark at start. Picnic areas and toilets at North Ledge and Fred Jacoby Park.*
On-site information: *Trailhead sign and yellow directional signs along the route.*
Best season: *Late winter and early spring for running water and wildflowers.*

NUMBAT

NUMBAT

The numbat (*Myrmecobius fasciatus*) is a small termite-eating marsupial that was once widespread throughout the open wandoo forest of the western Wheatbelt.

The banded anteater, as it is sometimes called, dines largely on termites and, before extensive clearing for agriculture and the introduction of the cat and the fox, was once widespread from Albany to Watheroo and east beyond Kalgoorlie to western New South Wales.

The numbat is a gentle and curious animal weighing up to half a kilogram and measuring about 20 centimetres in body length. Its fur is greyish and reddish brown with white flecks. Across the back and rump are tiger stripes of black and white. Its head is small and pointed, with white stripes above and below the eye and a black stripe through the eye.

Food is obtained by turning over sticks and branches on the ground, then rapidly licking up the exposed termites. Where termite galleries are close to the surface, the ground is dug up.

Two populations of numbats can be seen during the day in the Dryandra State Forest near Narrogin and the Perup jarrah forest, east of Manjimup. In these areas where fox numbers are controlled, numbats and other smaller mammals are becoming increasingly common.

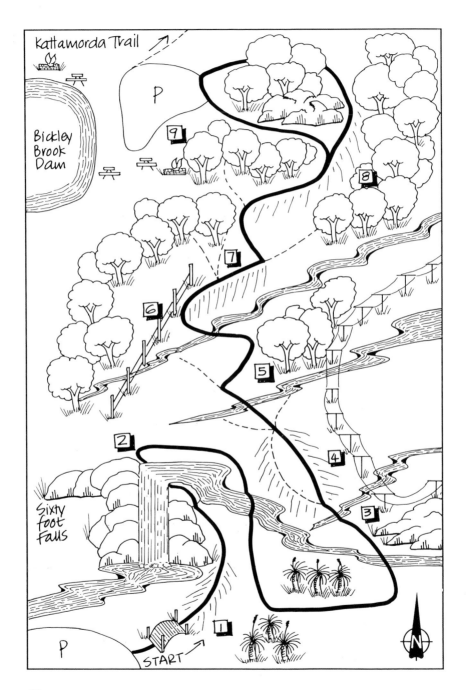

Kattamorda Trail

Bickley
Brook
Dam

P

9

8

7

6

5

4

3

2

Sixty
foot
Falls

1

P

START

N

54

Valley to Valley Walk

12

Ellis Brook

Length: *8 kilometres one-way*
Grade: *4*
Walk time: *3-4 hours*

This is a very pleasant one-way walk from Ellis Brook to Bickley Dam and you will need to arrange transport at the other end. The walk features wildflowers (in spring), jarrah forest, views over both valleys and rock outcrops. The last two or three kilometres is particularly attractive as you descend to Bickley Dam. The City of Gosnells organises an annual conducted walk along this route during the wildflower season (phone Recreation Services at the Council Offices for further details).

Note: Bickley Dam is a water catchment area and dogs are not allowed.

1   Starting from the carpark, cross the footbridge and follow the track along the creek to just past the first fork, where there are good views across to the falls. From here, there is a well-rewarded steep climb up to the falls.
2   There are delightful views looking over the valley towards the city from above the falls. Cross the creek, take a right turn and follow the track east along the edge of the creek. The track then crosses the creek and continues east until it meets a powerline, swings north to cross the creek once more and follows the powerline.
3   The large granite outcrop on your right makes a good spot for a rest and some refreshment. Take care not to damage the fragile vegetation growing on the rock.
4   After a short while, the track leaves the powerline and turns left to a ridgetop. Along this stretch are distant views over tree tops.
5   Just beyond the small creek, there are excellent views west over the city. Continue along the ridge and walk towards a wide creek ahead and fenceline on your left.
6   The track crosses the creek whose sandy banks are lined with old paperbarks and reeds.
7   At this point you get your first glimpse into the valleys that weave away to the east with a flush of green tree cover. Just beyond is a three-way intersection and you should take the track to the north-east. Turn left at the next main intersection and right at the one after that.

8   Standing on the ridgetop, surrounded by attractive dense jarrah forest, you have excellent views over Bickley Valley. Continue along the track with the rock outcrop to your right. After passing the rock you have a clear view down the valley.
9   Bickley Dam. Lunch beside the dam is a pleasant end to an enjoyable walk.

Fiona Marr and Tracy Churchill

Where is it?: *25 km south of Perth, access is from Rushton Road.*
Travelling time: *45 minutes from Perth.*
Facilities: *Carparks at both ends (check closing time), BBQs and tables at Bickley Dam.*
On-site information: *Silver trail markers in places along route.*
Best season: *Autumn, spring for wildflowers.*

WA CHRISTMAS TREE

CHRISTMAS
TREE

Western Australia is lucky enough to have its own Christmas tree, a mistletoe, which in early summer bursts into a profusion of brilliant orange flowers and heralds the approaching festive season.

The WA Christmas tree (*Nuytsia floribunda*) is botanically an unusual tree. It has no close relatives and is classed in a genus by itself. As a tree it is unlike all other mistletoes, which grow on the branches of trees.

The tree usually has a well-developed trunk that becomes very thick in relation to the tree's size. The branches are also thick and bend under the weight of the blue-green foliage and terminal flowers. The trunk of the tree, however, is not true wood, but a starchy tissue that is often gnawed by farm animals, sometimes right through.

WA Christmas trees are semi-parasitic. Their roots make rings around the roots of nearby trees and suckers within the rings extract water from them.

New plants can sprout from a large network of underground stems. As a result, groups of saplings are often seen around natural specimens.

The WA Christmas tree ranges from Kalbarri to Israelite Bay. It is common in almost all soil types on the coastal plain, particularly in low-lying areas. In the Darling Range, it grows chiefly in rocky or damp places.

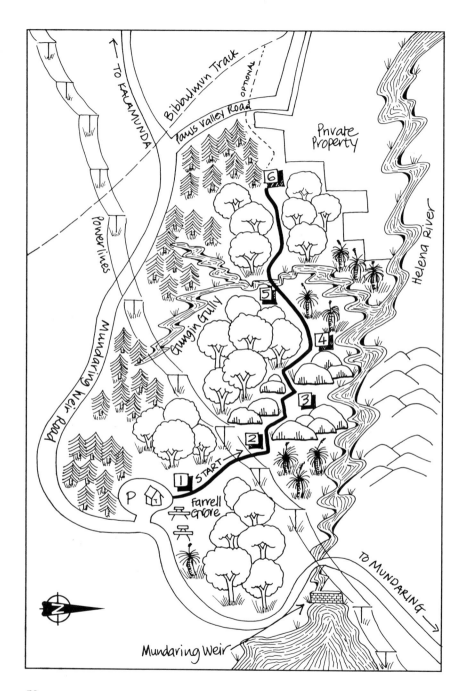

Winjan Track

Length: *14.4 kilometres return (plus options)*
Grade: *4*
Walk time: *3 hours*

This walk provides good views of Mundaring Weir and the Helena Valley. You may walk the entire length and return to Farrell Grove or follow the Bibbulmun Track to a waiting vehicle on Mundaring Weir Road (approx. nine kilometres total). Alternatively, you can walk to point 5 on the map then return to Farrell Grove (approx. eight kilometres total).

1   Leaving Farrell Grove picnic area, walk across the contour of the breakaway down into the Helena Valley. The forest is jarrah-marri woodlands with patches of regrowth forest. In parts, the understorey is dense blackboy and banksia with the forest floor laden with native grasses.

2   On arrival at the powerline there is a partially obstructed view of the Mundaring Settlement and the Devenish Pine Plantation only a few kilometres away on the other side of the Helena valley.

3   Here, the narrow path takes a turn left onto an old track which runs just below the ridge top on the southern slope of the valley. Soon, an open granite rock surrounded by pale bark wandoo provides panoramic views of the northern slopes. The sunlight reflecting off water on rocky outcrops opposite provide a tranquil setting for a short rest.

4   Further on you can look back to see the O'Connor Museum and the dark grey wall of Mundaring Weir. The path bends westward and opens up onto new views of green cleared paddocks and iron roofs of farm buildings set into the hillside. The path appears to divide the silver bark of the jarrah on the ridge top and the pale bark of wandoo on the upper slopes. Please take care not to disturb the vegetation in this area. It is an extremely diverse and fragile environment.

5   The track drops down into Gungin Gully. Downstream from where it crosses the creek there is a series of small waterfalls and cataracts. The gully and surrounding slopes provide one of the best spring wildflower displays in the area. You may choose to return from here to Farrell Grove.

6   If you decide to continue, the track leaves Gungin Gully and passes through interesting jarrah forest for a further three kilometres before linking with the Bibbulmun track, just east of Kalamunda National Park.

Jamie Ridley

Where is it?: *Farrell Grove, 40 km from Perth via Mundaring Weir Road.*
Travelling time: *1 hour from Perth.*
Facilities: *BBQs, toilets, tables, carpark.*
On-site information: *Trailhead sign and directional signs along the route.*
Best season: *All year except hot days, spring for wildflowers.*

NEW ZEALAND ADMIRAL

The North Walks 14 - 31

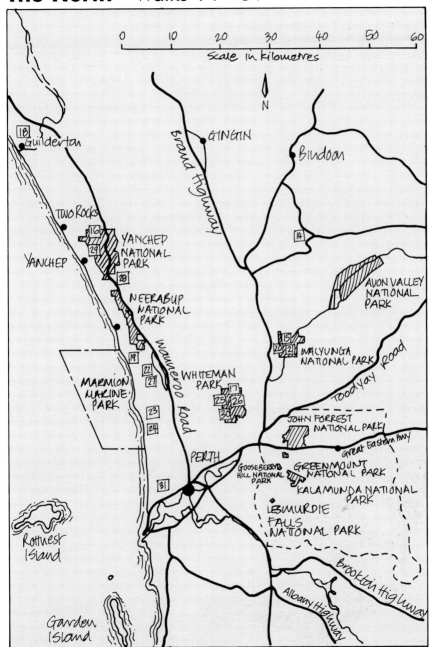

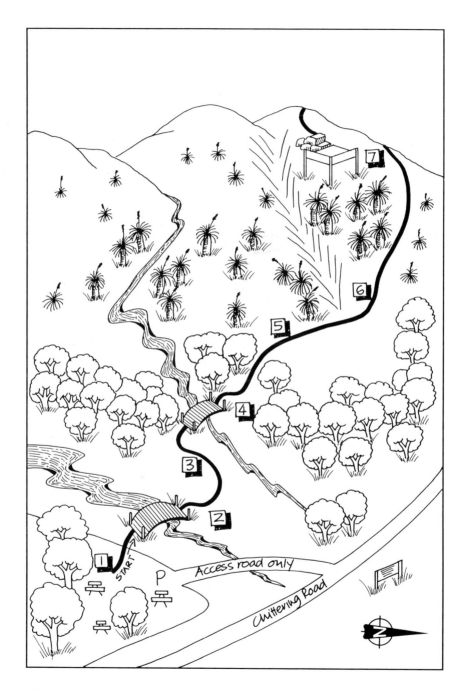

Blackboy Ridge Walktrail

Length: *1.5 kilometres return*
Grade: *1*
Walk time: *45 minutes (with stop at lookout)*

This pleasant walk is good at any time of the year, but it is truly spectacular during early spring when wildflowers are abundant. The hillside is covered with wattles, parrotbush, delicate orchids and, of course, hundreds of blackboys, which give the area its name. The trail follows a well-worn route that rises steadily up the hillside to a lookout.

1   Start from the north end of the small picnic area, where there is a wooden 'walktrail' sign.
2   Very soon you will cross a footbridge over a small creek.
3   The lower slopes of the ridge support a marri-wandoo woodland with its attendant understorey of heath plants.
4   A second footbridge crosses a very small creek which is dry for most of the year.
5   The marri-wandoo woodland thins out and heath vegetation becomes more dominant as you climb the gentle slope of the trail. The upper slopes are dominated by blackboys.
6   Looking uphill to the left of the track is a depression in the hillside, which is covered in blackboys and looks particularly attractive in spring.
7   On the final ascent, the trail passes briefly around the side of the ridge before crossing the summit and leading down to a lookout. From here there are spectacular views across the Chittering Valley.

David Gough

Where is it?: *70 km north of Perth in the Chittering Valley.*
Travelling time: *1 hour 20 minutes from Perth.*
Facilities: *Picnic area, carpark.*
On-site information: *Signs from road and carpark.*
Best season: *All year, spring for wildflowers.*

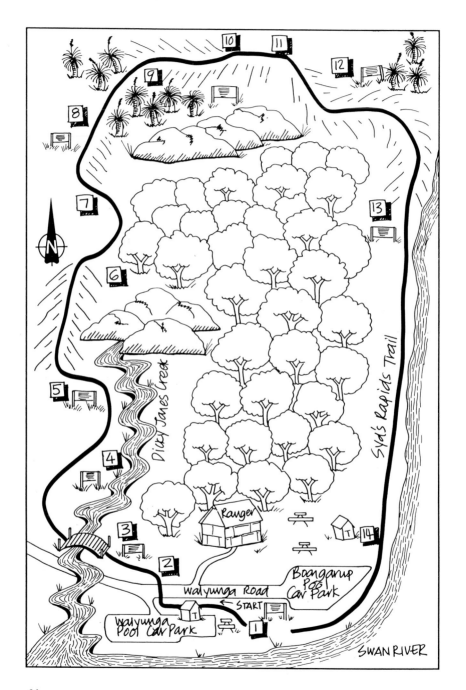

10

11

12

9

8

7

6

13

N

5

4

Dicey Janes Creek

Syd's Rapids Trail

3

2

Ranger

T

14

Boongarup Pool Car Park

Walyunga Road

START

1

Walyunga Pool Car Park

SWAN RIVER

64

Echidna Trail

15

Walyunga National Park ($)

Length: *10.6 kilometres loop*
Grade: *5*
Walk time: *4 hours 30 minutes*

This trail, which was made possible with assistance from Rotary International, offers walkers the chance to enjoy a variety of wildflowers at close quarters. There are some interesting granite outcrops and, although most of the trees in the area are wandoo and marri, you will see some small stands of jarrah on the high laterite ridges.

1 The trail begins as the Kangaroo Trail in the carpark at Walyunga Pool.
2 Follow the kangaroo markers and cross over the road into wandoo-marri woodland.
3 Cross Dicky Jones Creek for information about an old dwelling that was in the area.
4 At the start of the Echidna Trail there is an information panel about walktrail options. Follow the pink Echidna Trail markers.
5 Information panel near wandoo tells how the tree provides a habitat for numerous animals and birds.
6 This spot provides scenic views over the valley and photographic opportunities.
7 This spot overlooks the Swan Coastal Plain providing sweeping views.
8 At the junction with the Kingfisher Trail there is another information panel with details of walktrail options.
9 The information panel in Dicky Jones Gully tells the story of the Aboriginal significance of the area. Many large blackboys can be seen here.
10 Woodsome Hill, the highest point in the park at 260 metres above sea level, is clearly visible. An information panel gives more details.
11 This is another good spot for views across the Avon Valley.
12 As the trail descends to the river, the railway line which runs through the Avon Valley becomes visible. An information boards gives more details.
13 At this point, the Echidna Trail joins Syd's Rapids Trail and continues along the river's edge. An information panel gives details of how the rapids got their name.
14 Syd's Rapids Trail joins the Aboriginal Heritage Trail, which runs back to the start at Walyunga Pool picnic area. Interpretive panels along the trail give details of the Aboriginal heritage values of the park.

Ross McGill

Where is it?: *40 km north-east of Perth via the Great Northern Highway and Walyunga Road.*

Travelling time: *1 hour from Perth.*

Facilities: *BBQs, toilets, water at both picnic areas in the park.*

On-site information: *Trailhead sign, pink 'echidna' markers and interpretive panels.*

Best season: *All year except hot summer days, spring for wildflowers, winter for fast-flowing river.*

ECHIDNA

One of the world's most primitive mammals is widely distributed throughout Australia and inhabits outer urban areas of Perth.

The short-beaked echidna (*Tachyglossus aculeatus*), recognisable by its covering of long spines, has been seen waddling down suburban streets in Woodvale and turns up occasionally in backyards of Kalamunda and Armadale.

The echidna is one of only two Australian monotremes, or egg-laying mammals; the other is the platypus.

Female monotremes lay a soft-shelled egg and suckle their young on milk secreted through numerous ducts opening onto the abdomen. The egg is probably laid directly into the pouch on the belly of the female. There it hatches after ten days and the young remains there for a further three months.

A highly specialised feeder, the echidna exposes termite galleries by breaking open nests with its strong forepaws or snout or digging into soil, and extracts termites with its long sticky tongue.

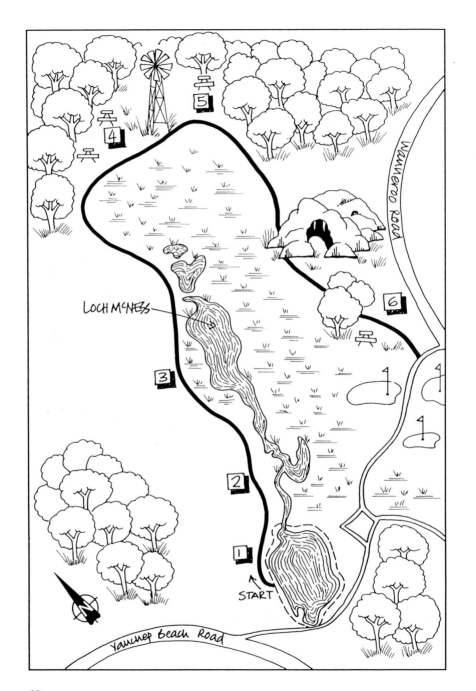

Ghost House Walk

16

Yanchep National Park ($)

Length: *11 kilometres circular*
Grade: *4*
Walk time: *4 hours*

The Ghost House Trail offers some of the best 'wilderness' walking in Yanchep National Park. It starts and finishes at the McNess House Visitor Centre and, for its first part, runs along the Yanjidi Trail before turning off to the left and continuing along the western side of the Loch McNess lake system. The trail passes through beautiful examples of tuart forest, banksia woodland and coastal heathland. Limestone outcrops are visible flanking the beautiful north lake on the north-west section of the trail, and walkers can search for the lost ruins of the 'Ghost House' on the northern side of the lake. A night walk is the best way to appreciate the magic of the tuart forest. Night life abounds in this area providing a symphony of nature.

IMPORTANT: Please register at the McNess House Visitor Centre before commencing this walk and check back in on your return.

1 Beautiful examples of tuart forest can be appreciated at this point. The trees are very old and many forms of life can be discovered within the loose, craggy bark.
2 Good examples of coastal heath. Wildflowers abound here in the spring.
3 Limestone outcrops on the east side of the lake are visible, flanking the bulrushes of the north lake wilderness area.
4 The 'Ghost House' ruins can be explored, but please do not disturb or remove anything found there.
5 Rough, rocky limestone ridge. Many invertebrates and reptiles live among the rocks.
6 Tuart forest.

Therese Jones

Where is it?: *Yanchep National Park, 51 km north of Perth on Wanneroo Road.*
Travelling time: *1 hour 10 minutes.*
Facilities: *Picnic area, toilets, carpark in the park.*
On-site information: *Directional signs along trail.*
Best season: *All year except hot summer days.*

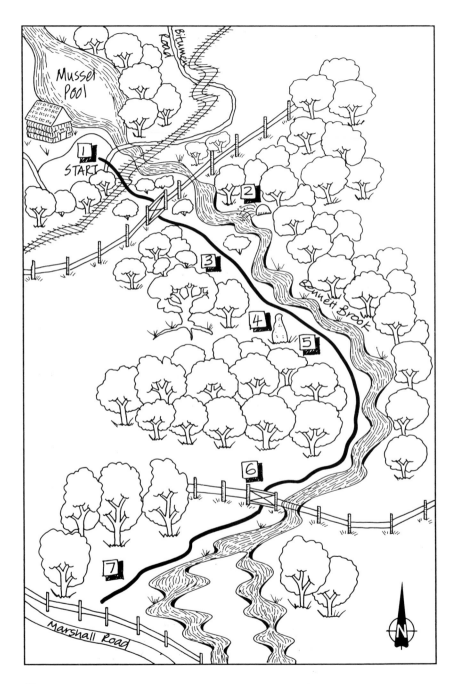

Goo-loorto Walktrail

17

Whiteman Park ($)

Length: *3 kilometres return*
Grade: *2*
Walk time: *1 hour 15 minutes*

'Goo-loorto' means a species of eucalypt (probably flooded gum) in the Nyoongar language of the area. This trail takes you along a running brook past a constant spring. Some waterbirds may be seen during winter and/or spring.

1   Starting at the log cabin by Mussel Pool, the first 200 metres of the trail passes through a thick grove of marris, flooded gums (*Eucalyptus rudis*) and paperbarks before crossing tram tracks and proceeding towards a gate. After passing through the gate, the trail follows the brook and tree line.
2   On the eastern side of the brook is a natural spring with edible watercress growing in the outflow. A fallen paperbark spans the brook.
3   A very old paperbark (*Melaleuca preissiana*) with a gnarled trunk stands back a little way from the brook. It has a girth of about seven metres and a diameter of just over a metre.
4   Here you can see an old ants' nest in the base of a marri tree.
5   The trail cuts up to the edge of the tree line. On the right is a grove of golden wattles (*Acacia saligna*), whose profuse yellow flowers can be seen in August and September. The trail passes several very old, multi-branched flooded gums.
6   Passing through a second gate, the trail passes into an area with only a few scattered paperbarks and marris that were left when land was cleared for grazing. The ground near the brook is low-lying and swampy, with watercress and bulrushes.
7   The trail ends at the Marshall Road fence line. From here you should return along the same route to Mussel Pool, where you can enjoy a barbecue.

Information supplied by Whiteman Park staff

Where is it?: *18 km north of Perth. Entrance off Lord Street, West Swan.*
Travelling time: *25 minutes from Perth.*
Facilities: *BBQs, tables, toilets, carparks, picnic shelters.*
On-site information: *Trailhead sign, red painted posts along trail.*
Best season: *All year, flowing brook winter to mid-summer, shady and cool in summer.*

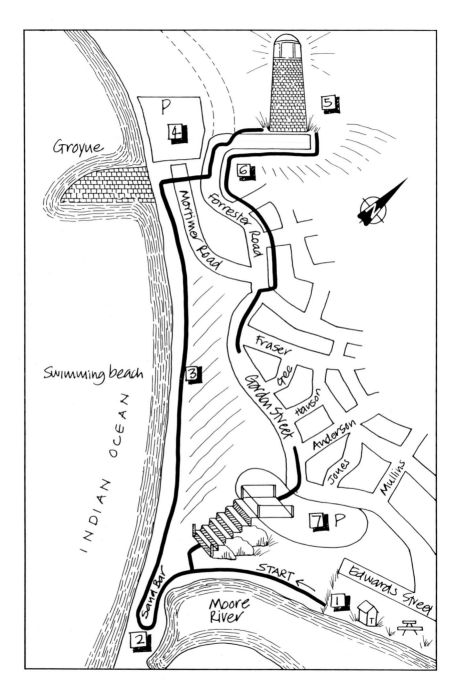

Groyne

Swimming beach

INDIAN OCEAN

P
4

P

5

6

Mortimer Road

Forrester Road

Fraser

Gee

Hanson

Gordon Street

Anderson

Jones

Mullins

3

7 P

Sand Bar

Moore River

START ←

1

2

Edwards Street

T

Guilderton Lighthouse Trail

18

Length: *4.3 kilometres loop*
Grade: *2*
Walk time: *2 hours*

The trail runs from the main picinic area, along the river and beach up to the impressive red-bricked lighthouse that stands high above the limestone cliff.

1 Starting from the picnic area, proceed along the river's edge to the sandbar at the mouth of the Moore River. There are very pleasant views across the river and to the ocean.
2 The Moore River is sealed by a sand bar at various times of the year, depending on seasonal rains. The sandbar usually closes the river mouth during the summer months and is generally passable except during high tides. Crossing should not be attempted at any time when the river is open to the sea.
3 Proceed along the beach heading north towards the groyne, which is clearly visible. This is a delightful stretch of beach that offers scenic grandeur and good swimming (when appropriate).
4 The groyne provides parking for vehicles and a boat launching facility. From here, climb uphill to Forrester Road and head towards the lighthouse.
5 The lighthouse is built in red brick to a height of 31 metres. There is no access into the lighthouse compound itself, but there are excellent views from Tank Road. Wildflowers abound during spring and you may see some bobtail skinks along the track.
6 Return along Forrester Road and Mortimer Road before turning into Gordon Street. This is also a good area for wildflowers in spring.
7 The lookout, near Gordon Street carpark, provides panoramic views over the ocean, the river and the Guilderton townsite. Walk down the steps to the beach and return to the picnic area via the riverside beach.

Richard Hammond

Where is it?: *97 km north of Perth. Picnic area in Edwards Street.*
Travelling time: *2 hours from Perth via Route 60 (Wanneroo Road).*
Facilities: *BBQs, playground, shelters, shop, toilets, caravan & camping sites.*
On-site information: *None, enquire at shop.*
Best season: *All year, spring for wildflowers.*

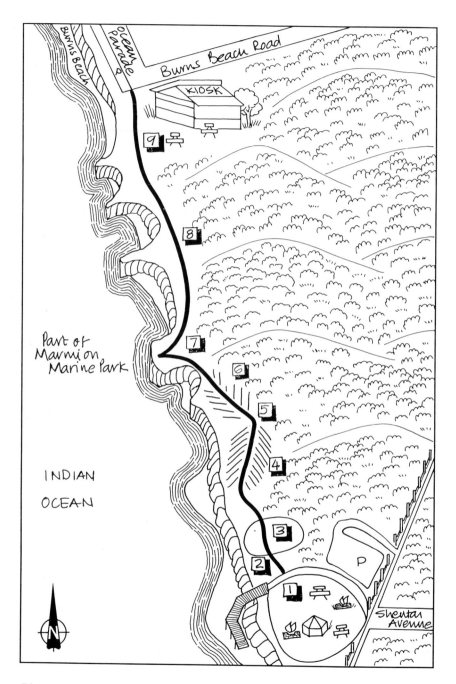

Iluka Foreshore Walktrail   **19**

Length: *4 kilometres return*
Grade: *2*
Walk time: *1 hour 30 minutes*

This is a pleasant clifftop walk from the recently established Beaumaris Beach picnic area, along the foreshore reserve between Iluka and Burns Beach. An informal trail, stretching from Ocean Reef to Quinns Rocks, has existed for some years, but this section has been formalised and there are plans for a number of recreational features including a cafe. The walk takes you through typical dune vegetation and provides uninterrupted views of the ocean.

1   The trail leaves Beaumaris Beach picnic area near the western end and heads north.
2   From here onwards you will see typical heath and dune vegetation including smokebush, parrotbush, rushes, wattles, grevilleas and a variety of pea plants.
3   This is the site of a proposed cafe and sunken gardens (1994-95).
4   Here you will see a number of other species including dune arctotheca, with its serrated paddle-shaped leaves, pigface and sea spinach.
5   From the top of this rise there are excellent views to the north and south, as well as inland across the foreshore reserve.
6   As you descent the northern slope of the rise, the limestone breaks through shallow surface soils.
7   The lookout point on the high limestone cliff provides excellent panoramic views.
8   Here there is access to a small sandy beach and a boardwalk is planned to make access easier. The vegetation near here is covered in dodder, a parasitic orange coloured vine.
9   At Burns Beach there is a shop and cafe, carpark and safe bathing.

Linda, Sarah and Cole Armitage

Where is it?: *26 km north-west of Perth at the west end of Shenton Avenue.*
Travelling time: *35 minutes from Perth via Marmion Avenue.*
Facilities: *BBQs, tables, shelter, carpark, cafe, shop.*
On-site information: *None.*
Best season: *All year.*

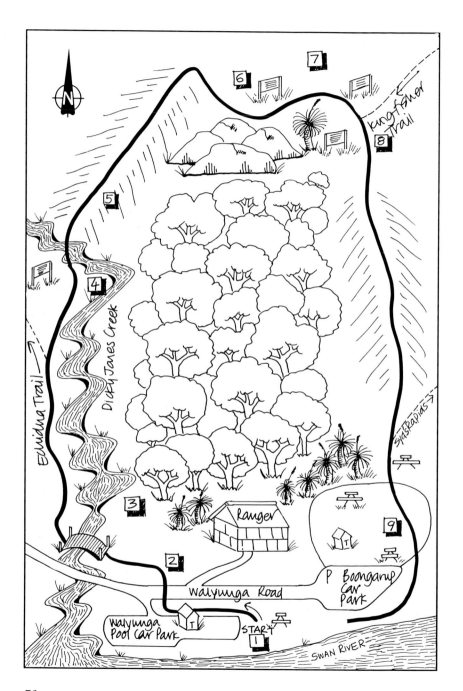

Kangaroo Trail

20

Walyunga National Park ($)

Length: 4 kilometres loop
Grade: 4
Walk time: 2 hours

This is the shortest of three walktrails installed in 1992 with assistance from Rotary International. It offers a range of vegetation types and in spring it is possible to find delicate orchids beside the track. Eucalypts flower in the summer and honeyeaters are attracted to the blossoms.

1   Starting from the Walyunga Pool picnic area, follow the yellow 'kangaroo' markers across the road.
2   This section is along an access track and moves steadily away from the road and into the wandoo-marri woodland.
3   Here, the trail crosses Dicky Jones Creek. There is an information panel giving details of an old dwelling that was in the area.
4   At the junction with the Echidna Trail is an information board giving details of trail options.
5   Crossing Dicky Jones Creek once again, the trail climbs uphill towards a granite outcrop.
6   Information panel about granite outcrops.
7   Information panel about blackboys.
8   Junction with the Kingfisher Trail. From here, the trail descends to the Boongarup Pool picnic area and the end of the Aboriginal Heritage Trail. Follow the Heritage Trail (in reverse) along the river's edge, which is lined with casuarinas and river gums, back to the Walyunga Pool picnic area.

Ross McGill

Where is it?: 40 km north-east of Perth along Walyunga Road.
Travelling time: 1 hour from Perth via the Great Northern Highway.
Facilities: BBQs, toilets, water, carparks at both picnic areas.
On-site information: Yellow 'kangaroo' markers and information panels along trail.
Best season: All year except hot summer days, spring for wildflowers.

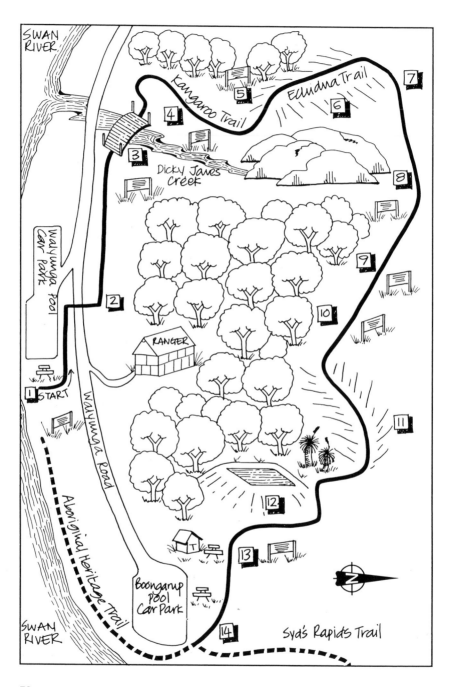

Kingfisher Trail

21

Walyunga National Park ($)

Length: *8.5 kilometres loop*
Grade: *5*
Walk time: *4 hours*

The first half of this trail follows the Kangaroo and Echidna Trails before branching off. This trail was completed with assistance from the Rotary International. The abundant wildlife and constant water supply in the present park shows why the Aboriginal people were so attracted to the area. Along the trail you will notice large ants' nests, giving further evidence of abundant nectar-producing plants.

1 Starting from the Walyunga Pool picnic area, follow the Kangaroo Trail and cross the road near the toilet block.
2 This section is along an access track and moves steadily away from the road and into the wandoo-marri woodland.
3 Here, the trail crosses Dicky Jones Creek. There is an information panel giving details of an old dwelling that was in the area.
4 At the junction with the Echidna Trail is an information panel giving details of trail options. Join the Echidna Trail and continue along it.
5 Here, an information panel gives detail about the habitats provided by wandoo trees.
6 At this point there are excellent views overlooking the valley and photographic opportunities.
7 When you reach this point the views are over the Swan Coastal Plain.
8 At this point, the Kingfisher Trail leaves the Echidna Trail and heads southwards following blue 'kingfisher' markers. An information panel gives details of trail options.
9 An information panel at this point gives details of wood borers found in wandoo trees.
10 An information panel at this point gives details of the process by which fallen trees are broken down through rotting and returned to the earth.
11 This spot provides views across the valley.
12 The large dam to the right of the trail provides water for park toilets and gardens.
13 Here, the Kingfisher Trail rejoins the shorter Kangaroo Trail and heads towards Boongarup Pool picnic area. An information panel gives details of walktrail options.

14 Here the trail joins the Aboriginal Heritage Trail and Syd's Rapids Trail. Follow the Aboriginal trail along the river and back to your starting point at Walyunga Pool picnic area.

Ross McGill

Where is it?: *40 km north-east of Perth along Walyunga Road.*
Travelling time: *1 hour from Perth via the Great Northern Highway.*
Facilities: *BBQs, toilets, water, carparks at both picnic areas.*
On-site information: *Trailhead sign, blue 'kingfisher' markers and information panels along trail.*
Best season: *All year except hot summer days, spring for wildflowers.*

MUSK DUCK

The musk duck (*Biziura lobata*) is found on most waterways and is usually seen floating motionless or kicking up great jets of water far from shore.

This bird is perhaps the most prehistoric, unduck-like looking creature found in our parklands. It has a blackish-brown plumage with numerous fine lines of light brown and floats very low in the water. Under the chin of the mature male is an unusual leathery bag.

During the breeding season, male musk ducks have an intense odour emanating from their oil or preen gland, which is situated on the birds' rumps. In courtship the birds stage a remarkable display by blowing out cheeks and neck, inflating their chin bag, spreading their spiny tail feathers over their back, throwing water and giving out a piercing, most unduck-like whistle with each kick.

As with other waterfowl, water levels determine breeding; so from the first rains in March through to September you are likely to see these individuals perform.

Musk ducks feed entirely by diving and can remain submerged for up to a minute as they search deep for aquatic insects, mussels, snails, crayfish and frogs.

The birds are entirely aquatic and are almost helpless on land. To escape detection they sink into the water leaving only their eyes and nostrils exposed.

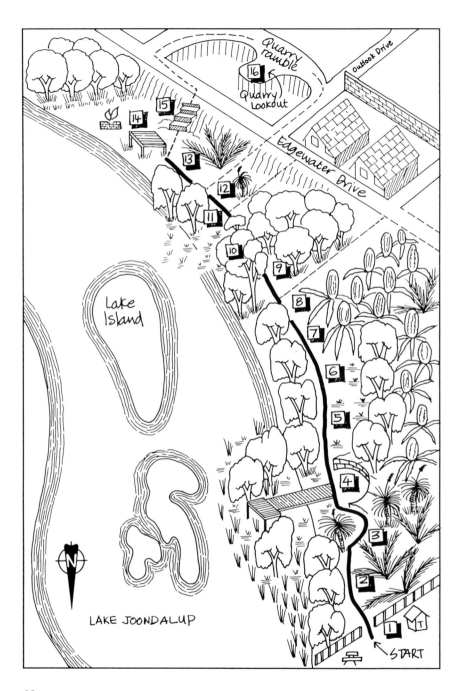

Lake Joondalup Nature Trail

22

Neil Hawkins Park

Length: *5 kilometres return (plus optional loop to lookout)*
Grade: *2*
Walk time: *2 hours (2 hours 30 minutes including lookout)*

This nature trail takes you along a limestone track south from Neil Hawkins Park by the edge of Lake Joondalup. It features paperbarks and rushes on the lake's edge and banksia-marri woodland in the drier areas to the west of the track. There is a gradual, but interesting change in vegetation types along the trail, which ends in a formal grassed area with basic picnic facilities by the lake's edge. There is an optional one kilometre loop to Quarry Lookout, which gives panoramic views across the entire lake.

1 Follow the limestone track at the south end of Neil Hawkins Park, where there are banksias and wattles.
2 Paperbarks and rushes dominate the lake edge on the left of the trail, while on the right are banksias, zamias, eucalypts and parrotbush. The trail is shaded by a canopy of trees.
3 Two large blackboys can be seen at the bend. The canopy begins to thin.
4 A boardwalk leads to an observation platform at the lake's edge.
5 Here, the paperbarks extend into swampy areas on both sides of the trail.
6 Groves of golden wattles form a canopy over the trail.
7 A large old banksia extends above the pathway.
8 To the right is a sandtrack that leads up through the woodland to Edgewater Road.
9 Wattles and melaleucas form a canopy over the trail.
10 Tall gums tower above the paperbarks on the left.
11 Here the canopy opens out to a swampy area with paperbarks on the left, wattles on the right and banksias on the far right.
12 Another sand track leads up to Edgewater Road.
13 The trail opens out to a paddock with zamias and occasional trees.
14 Picnic area with wood barbecue. From here you can retrace your steps or continue to Quarry Lookout.
15 Climb the steps and head south along the footpath. Cross Edgewater Road into Quarry Ramble and walk uphill on the right of the road.

16 Quarry Lookout provides magnificent panoramic views over the entire lake. From here, continue along Quarry Ramble, turn right into Outlook Drive then retrace your steps along the trail to Neil Hawkins Park.

David Gough

Where is it?: *Neil Hawkins Park, Boas Avenue, Joondalup, 25 km north of Perth.*
Travelling time: *40 minutes via Mitchell Freeway and Joondalup Drive. You can also travel by train to Joondalup and walk through Central Park to Neil Hawkins Park.*
Facilities: *BBQs, picnic tables, playground, toilets, carpark, large grassy area, bird observation platform.*
On-site information: *Trailhead sign.*
Best season: *All year.*

BANKSIA WOODLANDS

BULL BANKSIA

There are many species of banksia in Western Australia ranging from low-lying shrubs to large trees, and at least one species is in flower at any time of the year. The attractive flowers, clustered together in cylindrical, conical, dome-shaped or spherical heads, attract and support a wide range of insects, birds and mammals.

Six species of banksia occur as trees on the Swan Coastal Plain. They are generally found as banksia woodland with a rich understorey of macrozamias, blackboys, native shrubs, delicate orchids and a host of other wildflowers.

Firewood banksia (*Banksia menziesii*) has toothed leaves and yellow and orange-pink flowering spikes. Candle banksia (*B. attenuata*) has a narrow cylindrical cone of yellow flowers and narrow, slightly serrated leaves. The orange-flowered acorn banksia *(B. prionotes)* occurs on pockets of yellow soil. It can be found in Kings Park and on similar soils further north. The bull banksia (*B. grandis*) has leaves up to 40 centimetres long and occurs on grey sand, often with sheoaks. Holly-leaved banksia (*B. ilicifolia*) is a graceful tree superficially like candle banksia, but growing in even wetter ground around the perimeter of swamps and lakes. Its branches are long and erect with dark green holly-like leaves and flowers of cream and pink in a dome-shaped head.

85

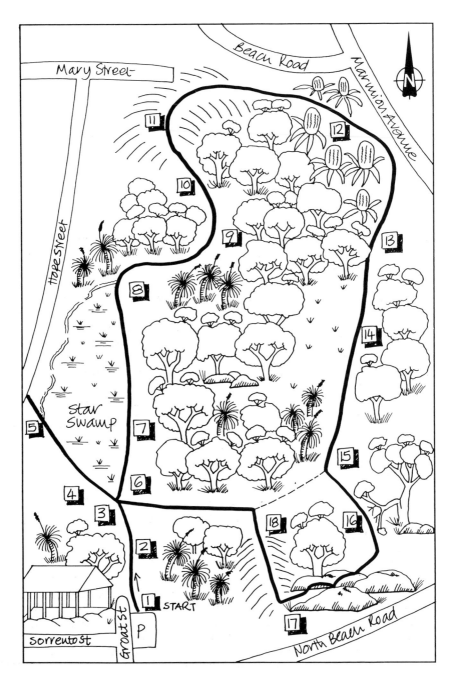

Star Swamp

23

Length: *4 kilometres loop*
Grade: *2 (accessible by wheelchair, except after heavy rain)*
Walk time: *1 hour 30 minutes*

Star Swamp Bushland Reserve is a 100 hectare nature reserve. The walk incorporates the Star Swamp Heritage Trail and native bushland just west of Marmion Avenue, passing through every vegetation type in the reserve. The area sustains a rich diversity of plant and animal life in tranquil settings and the walk offers opportunities for birdwatching and picnicking.

1 Starting at the Groat Street entrance, there is a large shelter built by Rotary International and a Heritage Trail sign. A very large, old tuart tree marks the start of banksia-sheoak woodland with orchids, pimelias and acacias.
2 On the left of the trail are two firewood banksias, one yellow and one red. There are also blackboys and native buttercups (*Hibbertia hypericifolia*).
3 The dead tuarts on the left are used for nesting by sacred kingfishers, galahs and 'twenty-eight' parrots.
4 The section of the trail from here to point 8 on the map is typical swamp-lake vegetation comprising paperbarks, white spray (*Logania* sp.), rare bitter bush (*Adriana* sp.), basket bush (*Spyridium* sp.), reeds and sedges. Birdlife includes white faced herons, ibis, ducks and nesting night herons. During winter and early spring you will hear the calls of many frogs.
5 In the mid-1800s cattle were driven down the Coastal Stock Route from Dongara to Fremantle. Star Swamp was one of many watering places en route. Original posts of an old stockyard can still be seen on the north side of the swamp.
6 The swamp was also a frequent watering hole for dairy cattle from the local Bettles Dairy, which closed in 1915.
7 Marl is a clay-like sediment that was used to seal limestone roads constructed in 1919 as part of the first housing subdivision. It was sometimes quarried from the swamp and evidence of this can be seen when the water level is low.
8 On the right of the trail is the first of the bull banksias (*Banksia grandis*) and a large spreading tuart tree with shrubland of prickly Moses (*Acacia pulchella*), *Grevillea vestita*, dwarf sheoak (*Allocasuarina humilis*), stinkwood (*Jacksonia* sp.) and blackboy. If you take the right fork in the track you will pass through a good stand of harsh hakea (*Hakea prostrata*), native wisteria (*Hardenbergia* sp.) with its bright blue flowers, and jarrah trees.

9   This section of track is all that is left of a major track that ran through the bushland in a south-easterly direction from Mary Street to North Beach Road. Here, the vegetation changes to tuart-jarrah-banksia woodland.

10 The vegetation changes again, this time to marri woodland. In late winter there are displays of white flowers on old man's beard (*Clematis pubescens*).

11 Up ahead is the Mary Street entrance with a Heritage Trail sign and map. This marks the end of the Heritage Trail and you should now turn right. There is a large bull banksia beside the Reserve sign and panoramic views to Duncraig.

12 Coming up to Marmion Avenue there is a large stand of acorn banksia (*B. prionotes*) on the left and on the right is candle banksia (*B. attenuata*) and the white star flowers of wedding bush (*Ricinocarpos glaucus*).

13 There are several dead tuarts on the left that are used as nest sites for corellas, galahs and 'twenty-eight' parrots. Looking right you see the old water tower, now a museum, on Mount Flora. Vegetation is tuart-banksia woodland and in late winter the understorey is a sea of yellow prickly Moses, with occasional scarlet runner (*Kennedia prostrata*) and native violet (*Hybanthus calycinus*).

14 Observation City Hotel can be seen straight ahead. The vegetation opens up to a heathland of parrotbush (*Dryandra sessilis*), native buttercup, one-sided bottlebrush (*Calothamnus quadrifidus*) and summer-scented wattle (*Acacia rostelifera*). White-cheeked honeyeaters can be seen on the parrotbush. Those wanting to stay on the limestone track (wheelchair users etc.) should cut through to point 17 on the map, otherwise follow the sand track to the left.

15 The sand track passes a large stand (approx 1 hectare) of *Grevillea vestitia*, with masses of pink and white flowers in late winter.

16 On the left is a tuart tree with a fallen branch. This is a good spot to look for blue fairy orchids in July and August.

17 The large tuart tree on the left marks a limestone outcrop with cockie's tongues (*Templetonia retusa*) and *Acacia truncata*, which together give a display of bright red and yellow flowers.

18 Meeting up with the limestone track, follow the Heritage Trail sign down the track through tuart-jarrah-banksia-sheoak woodland to point 2 on the map. Here you have a choice: you may return to the start at Groat Street or proceed to the lawned area in Hope Street (point 4 on the map) and have a picnic overlooking the lake and its waterbirds.

David Pike

Where is it?: *15 km north-west of Perth. Access is from Groat Street via Marmion Avenue, North Beach Road.*

Travelling time: *25 minutes.*

Facilities: *None.*

On-site information: *Trailhead sign, interpretive signs along Heritage Trail section only.*

Best season: *All year. Spring for wildflowers.*

FROGS

Frogs are amphibians. They begin life as tadpoles - a juvenile aquatic stage - before eventually becoming four-legged, air breathing adults.

Two families of frogs occur around Perth: tree frogs and ground frogs. Tree frogs are large, mottled brown or green and have circular discs on their toes. The bull frog (*Litoria moorei*) is between five and seven centimetres long and may have warty skin. The slender tree frog (*L. adelaidensis*), however, is between three and five centimetres long, smoother and wholly brown or green, except for a stripe along the body and red spots on the backs of the thighs. Both species live around wetlands and lay large masses of eggs, which are attached to vegetation at water level during spring.

Ground frogs have no circular discs on their toes and generally have warty skins. Some are only two or three centimetres long, while some lay eggs in water and others in burrows. The male moaning frog (*Heleioporus eyrei*) will construct a burrow and call the female to him.

All frogs are carnivorous. Small frogs have a predominantly insectivorous diet, but they also eat mites, snails, earthworms and spiders. Larger frogs may eat scorpions, centipedes, lizards and even smaller frogs!

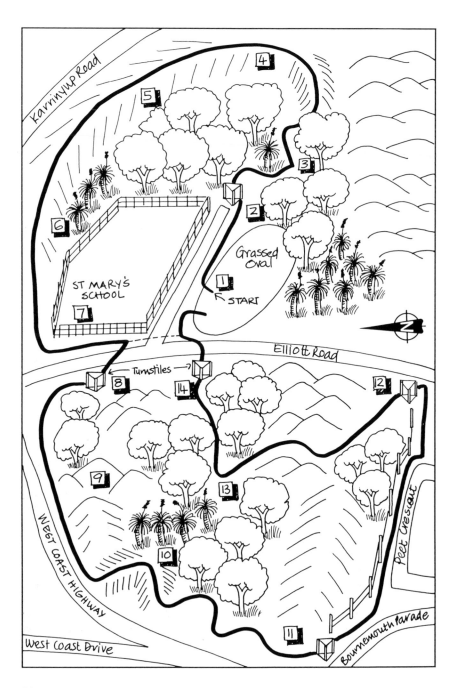

Trigg Bushland Trail   **24**

Trigg Bushland Reserve

Length: *5 kilometres loop*
Grade: *3-4*
Walk time: *2 hours*

This figure-of-eight trail takes you through one of the most important, but least well-known areas of natural coastal vegetation found anywhere in metropolitan Perth. It features views of the ocean and Rottnest Island, remnant groves of Rottnest cypress and tuart forest, abundant birdlife and masses of spring wildflowers.

1   Starting from Millington Reserve, just south of St Mary's School, walk along the access road and across the reserve to the edge of the bushland, keeping the school's cyclone fence on your left. You will pass some large tuart trees.

2   Enter the bushland through a turnstile. This is an open woodland of tuart with some acorn banksia. The understorey is mostly of one-sided bottlebrush and dune Moses, with some clematis and native wisteria. Proceed east on a lime-stone track.

3   Take the second left fork. There are dune sheoaks nearby. At the next fork turn right. Notice the replantings of Rottnest cypress. Carry on up the slope of the dune, keeping to the limestone track.

4   Keep left at the next junction. Here you are on the rim of one of the easternmost sand dunes of a major dune blowout system. The ocean is visible to the west and Rottnest Island will soon be visible on the horizon. Quandong, parrotbush, one-sided bottlebrush and coast daisy bush, with its blue leaves, grow here.

5   Continue west along the ridgeline through dune sheoaks and cross another track. Vegetation is more open because of recent fire. Corkybark, more often found in dry inland areas, and dune sheoak are regenerating on the northern slope. On your left you will pass a twisted specimen of corkybark.

6   Turn left at the next junction, then almost immediately turn right. This section passes between the perimeter fence of the school and the West Coast Highway.

7   You are now outside the bushland. Turn left and walk towards the school's main entrance and cross Elliott Road to the turnstile.

8   Follow the limestone track past summer-scented wattle and thickets of quandongs to a grove of tuarts in a sheltered area. The track climbs slowly (ignore the steep track on your left). You are now climbing one of the inner dunes of the dune blowout system.

9   Reaching the crest, you have a clear view of the ocean near Trigg Beach and of Rottnest Island on the horizon. The track descends past a thicket of parrotbush, which is very popular with birds such as white-cheeked honeyeaters. Turn right at the junction.

10 The track descends before curving away from the sea and climbing to a crest with Observation City Hotel visible behind dunes supporting groves of Rottnest cypress. Other cypress are close by on the ridgetop. It's thought that Rottnest cypress once covered extensive areas of the Swan Coastal Plain.

11 Before passing through the Bournemouth Parade turnstile, near West Coast Highway, you can see vegetation typical of coastal shrubland: fan flowers, spinifex, sword edge. From here you may decide to cross the highway to visit the beach before continuing your walk. Follow Bournemouth Parade inland and, around the corner, take the public footpath through to Peet Crescent and on to Elliott Road. Turn left and re-enter the bushland at the turnstile.

12 Turn right and follow the limestone track downhill, ignoring the left hand track at the bottom of the slope. Here is a sheltered area of tuarts, Rottnest cypress and summer-scented wattle. The track climbs steeply then descends through more wattle and patches of sword sedge.

13 Fig trees, water tanks and foundations mark the site of a house built in the 1930s as part of an unsuccessful subdivision. Turn right at the track junction.

14 After climbing through more wattle, turn right again at the next junction. This leads over the crest of a dune and descends to Elliott Road, opposite the access road to Millington Reserve.

Steve Tulip

Where is it?: *12 km north-west of Perth.*
Travelling time: *30 minutes via Karrinyup Road and Marmion Avenue.*
Facilities: *Off -road parking adjacent to Millington Reserve, Elliott Road.*
On-site information: *Maps of bushland at Bournemouth Road and Elliott Road entrances.*
Best season: *All year, spring for wildflowers, early mornings and evenings in warmer months.*

RATS AND MICE

BUSH RAT

Rodents (rats and mice) are usually thought of as being those 'uglies' that were introduced to Australia by Europeans. In fact, about five to ten million years ago, some species entered Australia from New Guinea and continued on an evolutionary course to occupy habitats from rainforest to deserts. These animals now have differing appearances as their environments have dictated physical change.

About a million years ago a new group arrived. These have also found diverse habitats but they still resemble typical Asian rats.

There are now 58 species ranging from the beaver-like water-rat (*Hydromys chrysogaster*) and the spinifex hopping-mouse (*Notomys alexis*) to the bush rat (*Rattus fuscipes*).

The domestic rats and mice that we often see in our towns and cities were introduced by Europeans some 200 years ago and have now spread out into natural habitats across much of the continent.

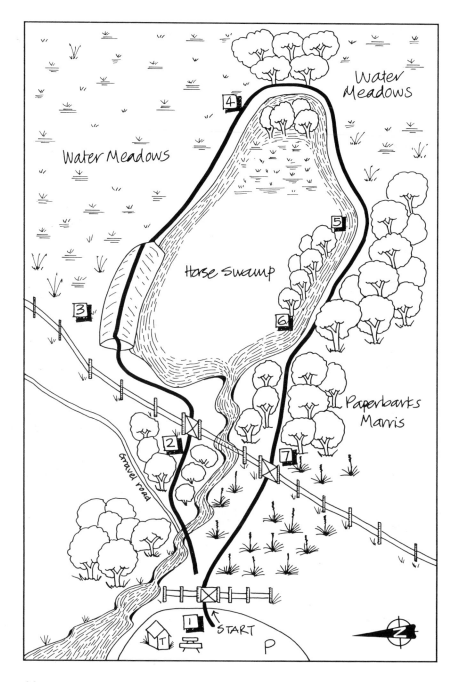

Water Meadows

Water Meadows

4

5

Horse Swamp

3

6

2

Paperbarks
Marris

Gravel road

7

1

START

T

P

N

94

Werillyiup Walktrail
Whiteman Park ($)

Length: *2.5 kilometres loop*
Grade: *1*
Walk time: *45 minutes*

'Werillyiup' means swampy place in the Nyoongar language of the area. The walk provides views across Horse Swamp and the opportunity to see a wide variety of birdlife. The trail begins at Bennett Brook carpark, 250 metres east of Mussel Pool.

1   Pass through the gate at the east end of the carpark. The trail runs along a gravel road and crosses the stream that feeds the swamp. Turn right off the road and head towards the next gate.
2   As you approach the gate the swamp is visible through the paperbark and marri trees. Walk through the gate and continue along the outside of the tree line (the trees stand in water during winter).
3   From the dam wall there are good views along the length of the swamp. Waterbirds are abundant at appropriate times of the year. From here to the eastern corner there are expansive water meadows on the left.
4   At the eastern corner of the swamp there is a very large stand of flooded gums (*Eucalyptus rudis*) on the left of the trail and paperbarks in the edge of the swamp on the right.
5   Along the southern edge there are good views back across the swamp before the trail passes through a grove of freshwater paperbarks (*Melaleuca raphiophylla*).
6   Here, the trail leaves the swamp and cuts through a thicket of paperbarks, stinkwood and marri.
7   Passing through the gate, the trail continues through a large area of blackboys (*Xanthorrhoea brunonis*).

Information supplied by Whiteman Park staff

Where is it?: *18 km north of Perth. Entrance off Lord Street, West Swan.*
Travelling time: *25 minutes from Perth.*
Facilities: *BBQs, picnic areas, toilets, water, carpark, restaurant.*
On-site information: *Trailhead sign, blue painted poles, interpretive signs.*
Best season: *Winter, spring, early summer.*

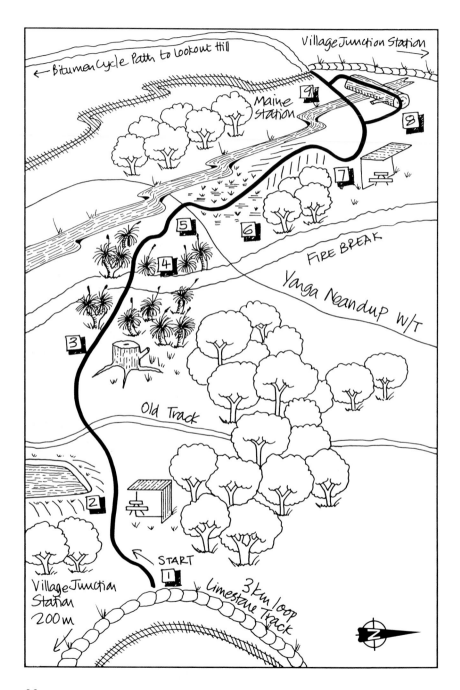

96

Wunanga Walktrail

26

Whiteman Park ($)

Length: *4 kilometres return*
Grade: *2*
Walk time: *1 hour 30 minutes*

'Wunanga' means quiet or peaceful in the Nyoongar language of the area. This trail takes you through an area of bushland encircled by the park's railway system. It passes through a variety of plant habitats and has two small picnic shelters.

1   The trail begins in open banksia-jarrah-marri woodland 200 metres north of Village Junction Railway Station off the limestone track marked '3 km Loop'.
2   A picnic shelter overlooks a small dam. About 200 metres further on the trail crosses an old firebreak track.
3   By the side of the trail is an old jarrah stump, known as the 'Black Stump Inn', that has been blackened by many bushfires. The trail passes through a grove of blackboys (*Xanthorrhoea preissii*), some of which have trunks of up to three metres and multiple crowns.
4   The trail crosses another firebreak and continues through the blackboys towards Bennett Brook.
5   The trail crosses Yonga Neandup Walktrail, marked with orange-topped posts.
6   Very soon you drop into a small, winter-wet swamp with several large paperbarks (*Melaleuca preissiana*), after which you climb up through a small patch of closed heath into open heath with blackboys and bracken. A line of paperbarks to the south-west marks the line of Bennett Brook.
7   Another small picnic shelter that overlooks open heath with blackboys.
8   Here the trail divides. The left fork is the short route across the brook, which is only dry in late summer. The right fork takes you to the permanent brook crossing by means of a fallen paperbark log.
9   The trail ends at Maine Railway Station. There is a choice of return routes.
    i)   Return along the same route back to the village (about a 45-minute walk).
    ii) Turn right and follow the limestone track to Village Junction Railway Station (about a one-hour walk).
    iii) Go straight on, turn left along the bitumen track via Lookout Hill, then left again along a limestone track to Village Junction Railway Station (about a one-hour-and-thirty-minutes walk).

Information supplied byWhiteman Park staff

Where is it?: *18 km north of Perth. Entrance off Lord Street, West Swan.*
Travelling time: *25 minutes from Perth.*
Facilities: *Picnic shelters. BBQs, carpark, toilets, restaurant in the village.*
On-site information: *Trailhead sign, yellow-topped posts along route.*
Best season: *All year, spring for wildflowers.*

SNAKES

When out walking during warm weather, around the block or through local parks or wetlands, you may cross paths with a snake.

But there's no need to panic. The fact that wildlife exists on these walks makes them educational and fulfilling. The truth is, snakes are more afraid of you and if you walk normally and boldly, most will sense your approach and move off.

The more commonly occurring of the venomous snakes found in the Perth Outdoors area are the front-fanged dugite and tiger snakes.

The dugite (*Pseudonaja affinis*) is olive brown or dark brown and may have odd black spots. This snake is fond of mice.

The western tiger snake (*Notechis scutatus occidentalis*) is an aggressive and dangerous reptile. It can be recognised by its rather stout form, broad head and dark blackish colour with or without a large number of pale orange-yellow cross bands. The under surface is usually pale orange-yellow. It prefers damp swampy situations where frogs abound and, at times, takes small lizards, mammals and birds.

If you are unlucky enough to be bitten by a snake, information on the treatment of snake bites is given in the 'Walking Safely' section at the front of this book.

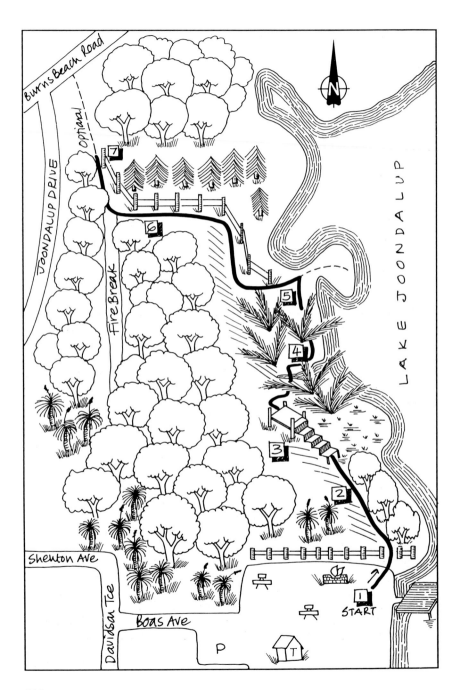

Yaberoo Budjara Heritage Trail

27

Stage 1 - Lake Joondalup

Length: *4 kilometres return*
Grade: *2*
Walk time: *1 hour 45 minutes*

This is the first stage of the 26 kilometres Heritage Trail from Lake Joondalup to Loch McNess, in Yanchep National Park. It provides a mix of wetland and dune vegetation.

1   The trail begins at the north end of Neil Hawkins Park, which was developed as a picnic area in 1979. Prior to then, the area had been a scout camp for a number of years.

2   Between the park and the lookout you can see two very different vegetation types on opposite sides of the trail. Along the lake's edge on the right are paperbarks, some flooded gums, bulrushes and sedges, while on the left side are tuarts and marris running up the ridge, and banksias and dryandras on the flat.

3   The mud near the base of the steps is about three to four metres deep and very dangerous. Walk up the steps to the lookout, from where there are excellent views across the lake. From the top of the lookout, follow the track down the slope to the lake's edge once more and cross a narrow channel.

4   Close to this spot are several caves. According to Aboriginal legend, a woman went to Malup Island, ignoring warnings about its sacred nature. This angered the *Waugal* (Rainbow Serpent), who dragged her through these caves to the sea. Early European settlers attempted to drain the lake's water into the caves, which has made them unsafe to enter.

5   The proliferation of zamias on the left side along this part of the trail gives it a prehistoric feel. However, there are introduced grasses - evidence of clearing at some time. Just before the trail heads uphill there are several fine peppermints. The paperbarks, flooded gums and sedges continue along the lake's edge, and from them the sounds of frogs calling to their mates can be heard during winter.

6   After passing the entrance to private property, the trail continues east. From here there are good views of the northern parts of the lake. At the 'T' junction with a firebreak, turn right and head towards Joondalup Drive.

7   The heritage trail continues along Joondalup Drive to Burns Beach Road. However, you may stop at Joondalup Drive and return to Neil Hawkins Park.

David and James Gough

Where is it?: *Neil Hawkins Park, Boas Avenue, Joondalup, 25 km north of Perth.*

Travelling time: *40 minutes via Mitchell Freeway and Joondalup Drive. You can also travel by train to Joondalup and walk through Central Park to Neil Hawkins Park.*

Facilities: *BBQs, picnic tables, playground, toilets, carpark, large grassy area, bird observation platform.*

On-site information: *Trailhead sign, marker arrows along trail.*

Best season: *Autumn, winter, spring.*

BOBTAIL SKINK

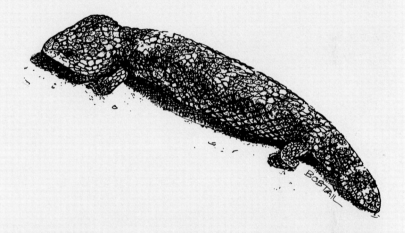

Skinks are one of the largest families of lizards, both in Australia and overseas, and about half of all Australian species are found in Western Australia.

The bobtail skink (*Tiliqua rugosa*) is probably the most commonly seen reptile in the Perth Outdoors area. These stout, scaly, stumpy-tailed skinks are more commonly seen in open habitats like roads and rock outcrops, whereas the slender, shiny-skinned smaller species of skinks prefer leaf litter, or other places with more cover.

The colouration of the bobtail skink is very variable. Commonly, the head and back are orange-brown to brown with creamy spots, blotches or streaks. The belly is white, creamy or grey with blackish fleck, spots or blotches.

If approached, a bobtail will often open its mouth wide and display its prominently coloured tongue in an aggressive stance. However, they pose no threat to humans.

Unfortunately, these slow-moving creatures are often found dead on the roads.

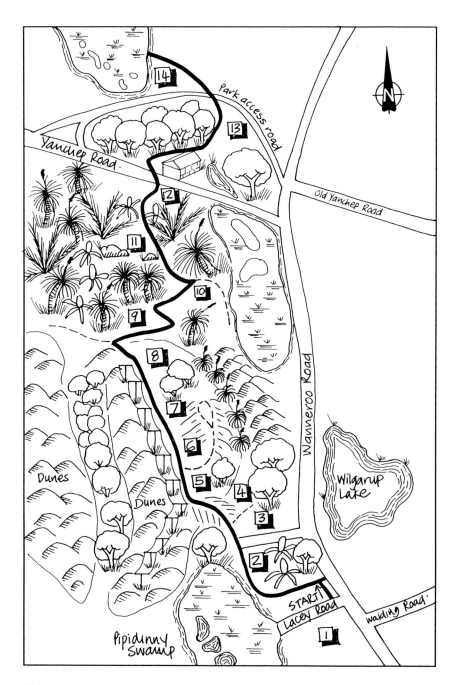

Yaberoo Budjara Heritage Trail

28

Stage 5 - Pipidinny Swamp to Loch McNess

Length: *5.2 kilometres one-way*
Grade: *3 (some loose sand)*
Walk time: *2 hours 30 minutes*

This walk begins at the southern end of Yanchep National Park and takes you through a part of the park that is seldom explored by visitors. It features marked changes in vegetation types, excellent views over the dune system and is particularly attractive in spring. This walk is best done in the morning and walkers should be dropped at the start and met, ideally with a barbecue lunch, at the lake side.

1 The walk begins at the junction of Lacey Road and Wanneroo Road. The trailhead sign is in a hollow on the north side of the road. From here you wind between banksias until you reach a management track. Turn left and proceed to the fence.
2 Follow the fence line north. On the right of the track is banksia and marri woodland, while on the left is the swamp. Aboriginal legend has it that the swamp was created out of the blood and meat from the tail of the Crocodile that settled here.
3 After passing a track to the right, the trail narrows slightly and winds into the woodland. On the left is a large grove of tuarts in a low-lying area adjacent to limestone ridges.
4 Continue along the trail until you meet another track. Take the left fork and climb a sandy slope towards the electricity pylons at the top of the dune.
5 At the top of the dune there are excellent views to the east. Follow the track north.
6 A short track, opposite one of the pylons, leads 50 metres to a high point with spectacular 360° views.
7 This section along the dune is typical coastal heath. There are a few blackboys between the dunes, but it is mainly low scrub of wattle and other heath vegetation.
8 This vantage point is the northern edge of the dune system. To the east is the depression that is part of the chain of wetlands running south from Loch McNess to Lake Joondalup and beyond. Walk down from the top of the dune.
9 Turn right at the junction by the base of the dune. This section runs on the edge of two vegetation systems - banksia woodland on deeper sands to the north and heath on the younger sands on the south.

10 Leaving the edge of the dunes, the track winds through very pleasant banksia woodland that features several banksia species, blackboys and zamias. At the 'T' junction, marked by a large curved blackboy, take the left track and continue north.

11 This section, which also features parrot bush, rises out of the woodland to more open heath vegetation with limestone rock pushing through the soil surface. You then drop down again to see more banksias.

12 As you cross Yanchep Road you will see the Beach House. The track passes on the left of the house and winds around it and through tuart trees towards the park road.

13 Off the track to the north is White's Grotto - a natural amphitheatre with a small cave off to one side. Permission must be obtained from the Park Office before entering caves.

14 Cross the park road and head towards Loch McNess. This lake is extremely significant to the Aborigines of the area. The lake itself is a Dreaming site, and the level ground of its south-east corner (now the main picnic area) was a traditional meeting, corroboree and ritual area.

David Gough

Where is it?: *Corner of Lacey Road and Wanneroo Road, 47 km north of Perth.*
Travelling time: *1 hour 10 minutes from Perth.*
Facilities: *BBQs, water, shop, hotel, toilets in the park.*
On-site information: *Trailhead sign and yellow markers along track.*
Best season: *Autumn, winter, spring for wildflowers.*

WESTERN GREY KANGAROO

WESTERN GREY
KANGAROO

These animals were once common throughout what is now the Perth metropolitan area. They can still be seen in small groups at dusk or dawn in the outer northern, southern and hills areas. A large population can be seen in the late afternoon browsing the fairways of the golf course at Yanchep National Park.

The western grey kangaroo (*Macropus fuliginosus*) is a marsupial. Its young are born in a very incomplete state - minute, blind, hairless and with hind limbs only partially formed. The defenceless young finds its way to the mother's pouch and attaches to a nipple where it develops fully over a period of about 42 weeks.

The male western grey kangaroo can grow to more than two metres from head to tail tip and weigh more than 50 kilograms. It has a strong characteristic odour, hence its nickname 'stinker'.

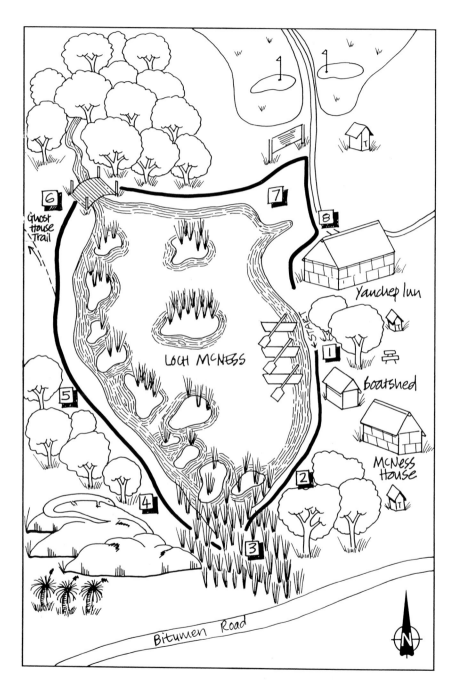

108

Yanjidi Trail
Yanchep National Park ($)

Length: 2 *kilometres circular*
Grade: 1
Walk time: 1 *hour 30 minutes*

This trail takes you through the heart of a coastal wetland, circumnavigating Loch McNess. Yanjidi is a variation of *yanget*, the Nyoongar Aboriginal word for the native bulrush that is a prominent feature of the walk.

1   Start from the Boatshed on the east of Loch McNess and proceed south along the lake's edge. Here you can see waterbirds, including the musk duck, and the occasional tortoise coming up for air.
2   The trail passes through thickets of acacia, which grew prolifically following a hot wildfire in 1991.
3   On the southern edge of the lake, the trail meanders through head-high sedges and rushes.
4   Heading up the western side of the lake you pass beneath overhanging paperbarks and you may see some lizards sunning themselves on limestone rocks.
5   Here, remnants of the most northerly tuart forest can be seen along the limestone outcrop. Night herons, ibis and cormorants drying their wings in the morning sunlight, are often seen at the lake edge. It is believed that Aboriginal groups congregated in this area, which is rich in natural food resources.
6   During the park's development in the 1930s, the lake was dredged of excess sedges and rushes. The remains of the dredger now form part of the bridge that crosses the lake at this narrow point.
7   The water supply that flows through the lake system comes from an underground water source called the Gnangara Mound.
8   The trail joins the road to the golf course. Turn right here, cross the water and follow the lake edge behind Yanchep Inn back to the starting point.

Therese Jones

Where is it?: Yanchep National Park, 51 km north of Perth on Wanneroo Road.
Travelling time: 1 hour 10 minutes.
Facilities: Picnic area, toilets and carpark in park.
On-site information: Trailhead sign, directional signs along route.
Best season: Spring, summer, autumn.

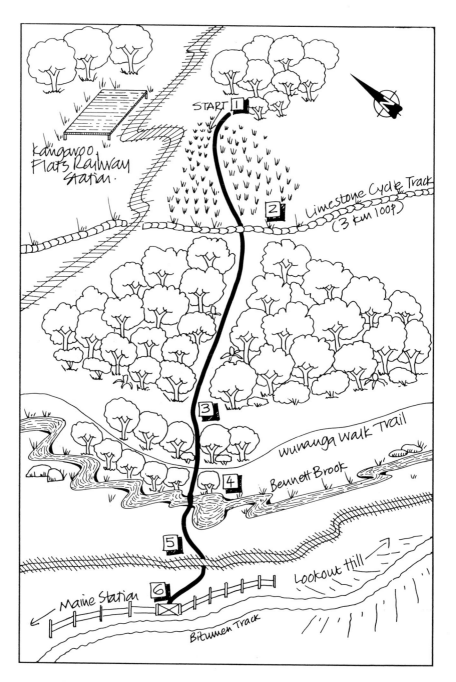

Kangaroo Flats Railway Station.

START [1]

[2] Limestone Cycle Track (3 km loop)

[3]

Wunauga Walk Trail

[4] Bennett Brook

[5]

Maine Station [6]

Lookout Hill

Bitumen Track

Yonga Neandup Walktrail   **30**
Whiteman Park ($)

Length: *3 kilometres return*
Grade: *1*
Walk time: *1 hour 15 minutes*

'Yonga neandup' means a flat open space where kangaroos can be found, in the Nyoongar language of the area. This trail winds through woodlands, rich in wildflowers during spring, and crosses various vegetation types. The trail begins at Kangaroo Flats Railway Station (about a kilometre from Village Junction Railway Station) and there are alternative return routes by foot or by train.

1　The trail leaves the station and crosses an area of low tufty sedge-like plants.
2　After crossing a limestone cycle track ('3 km loop'), the trail winds for the next 500 metres through a beautiful patch of banksia-jarrah-marri woodland. A wide variety of wildflowers can be seen, particularly between August and October.
3　Coming out of the woodland, the trail crosses a fire break. Fifty metres further on it crosses the Wunanga Walktrail, marked with yellow-topped pine posts. Masses of cowslip orchids (*Caladenia flava*) can be seen in September.
4　Cross over Bennett Brook. Small pools of water lie either side of the culvert.
5　Cross the railway tracks and follow an old firebreak surfaced with blue-metal.
6　The trail ends at the bitumen track. There are four return route options:
  i)　Return back along the same route to Kangaroo Flats Railway Station.
  ii)　Turn right along the bitumen track to Maine Railway Station (about a 10-minute walk) and catch a train to the village.
  iii)　Turn right towards Maine and continue on foot via the '3 km loop' cycle track to the village (about a one-hour-and-fifteen-minutes walk).
  iv)　Turn left along the bitumen track via Lookout Hill and Mussel Pool to the village (about a one-hour-and-fifteen-minutes walk).

Information supplied by Whiteman Park staff

Where is it?: *18 km north of Perth. Entrance off Lord Street, West Swan.*
Travelling time: *25 minutes from Perth.*
Facilities: *None at start of trail. BBQs picnic shelters, toilets, carparks, restaurant at the village.*
On-site information: *Trailhead sign, orange-topped posts along route.*
Best season: *All year, spring for wildflowers.*

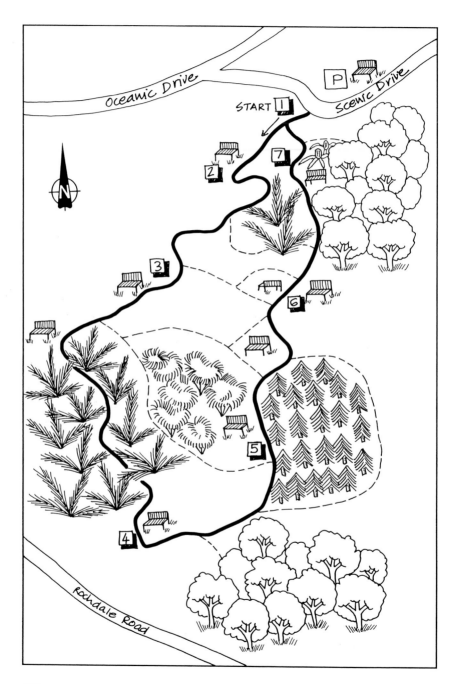

Zamia Trail

Bold Park

Length: *5 kilometres loop*
Grade: *3*
Walk time: *2 hours*

This walk begins at Reabold Hill and provides views to the ocean and inland as well as changes in vegetation types and abundant birdlife.

1   Starting at the lookout on Reabold Hill there are extensive panoramic views to Rottnest and Garden Islands, the Darling Range, Perry Lakes and Perth City. The trail heads downhill from the carpark.
2   A short way down the track on the right is a view trail to the first of several seats. From here there are good views to Rottnest Island. Vegetation along the trail includes banksias, kangaroo paws and acacias.
3   Thornbill Walk Lookout provides views over surrounding bushland of scattered tuarts with banksia understorey, and beyond to Cottesloe and Garden Island. This section features an abundance zamias which give the trail its name.
4   This is the site of an old turf farm. An open grassy area with freesias along the trail. Further on and to the south are stands of redhearts (*Eucalyptus decipiens*).
5   At the intersection with the Sheoak Walk is another bench. There is a pine plantation on the right of the trail and sheoaks on the left.
6   Another view trail to the left of the track takes you to a seat facing north and giving views over bushland. There are more zamias to be seen along this section to the left of the trail and narrow-leaved red mallees (*Eucalyptus foecunda*) on the right.
7   Here, the Zamia Trail meets Camel Lake Trail. There is a seat beneath a banksia tree.

Peter Sharp

Where is it?: *8 km from Perth off Oceanic Drive.*
Travelling time: *15 minutes from Perth.*
Facilities: *Carpark.*
On-site information: *Signs on access road and at trailhead, directional signs along trail.*
Best season: *All year, spring for wildflowers.*

The River   Walks 32 - 38

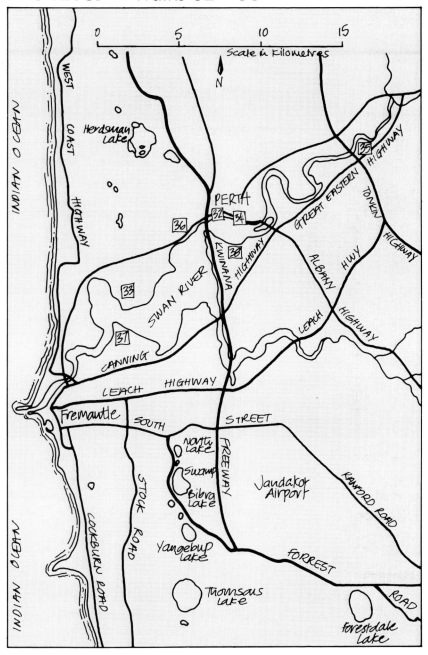

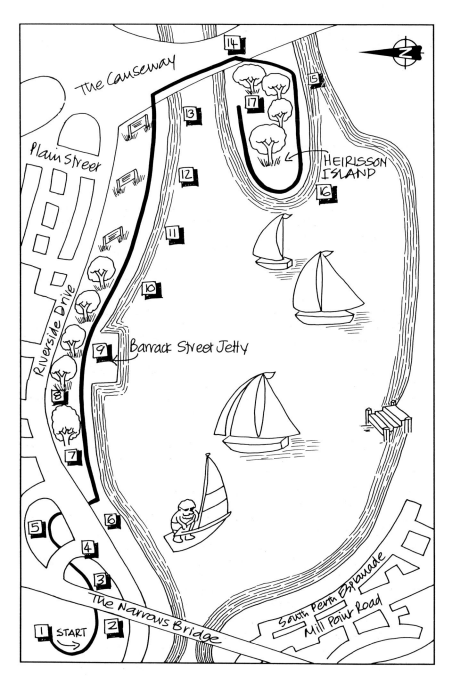

Between the Bridges Walk **32**

Perth Water

Length: *10 kilometres return*
Grade: *3*
Walk time: *3 hours*

This walk links the two major river crossings at each end of the city. It runs for much of its route along the water's edge and highlights the contrast between the busy city and the tranquil river. Except for Heirisson Island, the walk is along a dual-use cycle/walktrack and is suitable for wheelchairs, prams and strollers. It is best walked on a Sunday when there should be less traffic noise.

1   The walk begins at the small carpark by the ornamental lake and Narrows interchange in Mounts Bay Road. The Four Seasons Trail passes through here.
2   Walk south and pass under the Narrows Bridge. There are superb views down the river to the Old Swan Brewery and across to Mill Point and South Perth foreshore.
3   This small wetland, located within the narrows interchange, has the city skyline as a backdrop and is teeming with birdlife.
4   The first of three underpasses. This quiet space is a popular lunchtime retreat for nearby office workers who want to relax or read a book. Facilities here include a toilet block, drinking fountain and bench seating.
5   A small open space between three underpasses: one leading to the city, the second to the foreshore and the third back towards the brewery. A large information obelisk gives details about the construction of the freeway interchange and the river's geomorphology. Take the underpass to the river.
6   There is a nice focal view through the underpass to the river.
7   This part of the walk is dominated by river views to the south and the new TransPerth Bus Station to the north. Traffic noise can be intrusive, but the sound of waves against the river wall helps mask this a little.
8   The Four Season's Trailhead sign is just before Barrack Street Jetty. The trail, also in this book, runs to Kennedy Fountain.
9   Barrack Street Jetty serves as a departure point for river cruises, and ferries to South Perth and Rottnest Island. There is a kiosk and toilets.
10   The WA Rowing Club, classified by the National Trust, is an interesting old wooden building that was built around 1905.
11   From this point the city seems more removed, because of the large expanse of Langley Park. The park was Perth's first aerodrome. From time to time the park

is used to commemorate historical aviation events, which see dozens of vintage aircraft on display or flying. Other exhibitions and sporting events are also held here.

12 As you come to the junction of Plain Street and Riverside Drive, Heirisson Island (ahead) forms a pleasant backdrop and contrast to the residential developments on the South Perth foreshore.

13 The trail diverges from Riverside Drive and passes through a grassed public open space beside the river. Here there are cycle hire facilities, children's playground and a drinking fountain. The river narrows and Heirisson Island forms the dominant focal point. Walk onto the Causeway Bridge and head south.

14 Access to Heirisson Island is on the right, mid-way across the bridge. The pathways on the island are compacted limestone and are unsuitable for wheelchairs.

15 Walk to the south bank of the island. This part is a grassed open space with several internal wetlands and extensive clumps of trees. It is a popular spot for fishing and picnicking. Head around the western portion of the island in a clockwise direction.

16 The western end of the island gives superb views of Perth Water and the Narrows Bridge, with the city and Kings Park providing a picturesque backdrop. On a broad grassy knoll is a large bronze statue of the Aboriginal leader Yagan, whose people once inhabited areas by the Swan and Canning rivers.

17 The northern bank of the island is more open and susceptible to wind exposure. The city skyline and the lights of the WACA ground dominate the view across the narrow river channel. From here, continue to the Causeway Bridge and return to the carpark on Mounts Bay Road along the river foreshore. Walking in a westerly direction gives a different perspective with Kings Park becoming a more dominant feature.

Wayne Schmidt and family

Where is it?: *1 km from Perth city centre. Carpark just off Mounts Bay Road on the north of the Narrows.*

Travelling time: *5 minutes.*

Facilities: *Seating, water and children's play areas at various points along the walk.*

On-site information: *Four Seasons Trailhead sign at Barrack Street Jetty.*

Best season: *All year (Sundays for less traffic noise).*

CORMORANTS

One of the attractions of the Swan and Canning Rivers is the sight of cormorants perched on posts, boats and shoreline obstacles, often in heraldic poses, as they dry outstretched wings in the sun.

The little pied cormorant (*Phalacrocorax melanoleucos*) is the commonest of four species that inhabit our waterways on the west coast. This bird is medium sized at about 60cm long, with a black back, white underparts and yellowish beak.

Similar in size and habits and almost as common is the little black cormorant (*P. sulcirostris*), which is completely black. Little black cormorants are sometimes seen in flocks of a thousand or more fishing on the Swan River.

The two largest birds, at about 80 centimetres, are the pied cormorant (*P. varius*), similar in appearance to the little pied cormorant except for a yellow-orange face patch in front of the eye, and the black cormorant (*P. carbo*), the biggest of all the species.

Cormorants feed by diving, usually from the surface, and swimming under water for periods of up to half a minute or more. They are propelled by large webbed feet. At the surface they swim with alternating leg strokes, while underwater they use both feet together. Depending on where they feed, they prey on small fish, crustaceans, amphibians and insects.

As well as frequenting the Swan and Canning rivers, cormorants are also found on Perth's lakes and swamps.

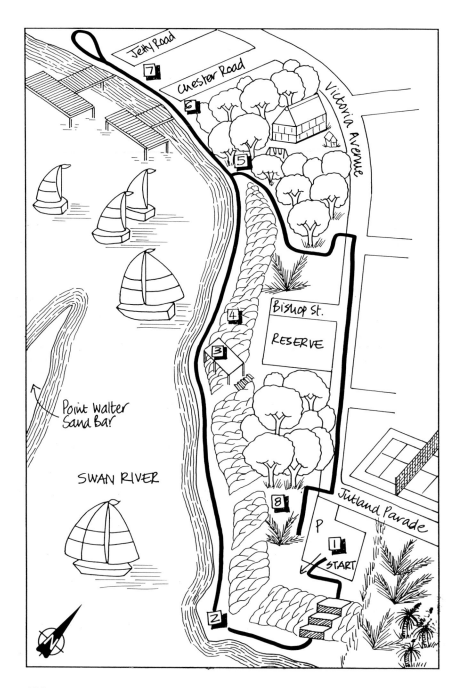

Jetty Road

Chester Road

7

6

Victoria Avenue

5

Bishop St.

RESERVE

4

3

Point Walter
Sand Bar

SWAN RIVER

8

Jutland Parade

P

1

START

2

N

Claremont Foreshore Trail

33

Length: *5 kilometres loop*
Grade: *3-4*
Walk time: *1 hour 30 minutes*

This walk offers a riverside experience with views across to Alfred Cove, Lucky Bay, Point Walter, Mosman Bay and Freshwater Bay. Parts of the walk offer a sense of what the river would have looked like to Captain Stirling as he sailed upstream from Fremantle.

1   From the small carpark adjacent to Point Resolution Reserve there are panoramic views of the river. A metal plaque indicates the point was named after the ship *Resolution* and was also the location of a convict depot. A limestone and concrete pathway runs down from the carpark to the river foreshore.
2   Downstream, the beach is mainly sandy, sometimes rocky and rarely wider than three or four metres. There are several other paths leading up to the reserve.
3   The low lookout (brick pillars supporting concrete roof) marks Bishop Road Reserve. A bitumen path leads up to the reserve.
4   About 100 metres further along the foreshore, the beach narrows to about one metre past tall limestone 'pinnacles'. Be sure to check the tide before continuing. The beach here is narrow, often rocky and frequently covered with reeds and grass. River views are excellent, but you need to stand still to enjoy them in case you stumble.
5   Here the foreshore widens to a grass reserve (Mrs Herbert's Park) with playground, trees and toilets halfway up the hill. Claremont Museum is at the top of the hill.
6   A foreshore reserve leads along to a small carpark at the bottom of Chester Road. A plaque on stone marks the site of the old Claremont Baths.
7   Claremont Jetty, on Jetty Road adjacent to Claremont YC. There are views to Keanes Point and the Royal Freshwater Bay YC and downstream to Blackwall Reach. From here, retrace your steps to Mrs Herbert's Park and visit the Museum before continuing south along Victoria Road.
8   Point Resolution Reserve contains a mix of native and eastern States trees and shrubs. At the northern end of the reserve is a clump of trees shading a brick paved circle with picnic table.

Ann Nicholson

Where is it?: *9 km south-west of Perth on the north bank of the Swan River.*
Travelling time: *20 minutes from Perth.*
Facilities: *Picnic area, tables, water, carpark.*
On-site information: *None.*
Best season: *All year - check tide times.*

BLACK SWAN

The black swan (*Cygnus atratus*) was first recorded by the Dutch navigator Vlamingh in January 1697 while in the Swan Estuary. Although it is to be found throughout Australia, this graceful bird has been regarded with special affection by many generations of Western Australians. It is the State's bird emblem and has long been used to identify things Western Australian.

Black swans can be seen on most waterways throughout the lower half of Western Australia. They frequent open areas of fresh, brackish and salt water like flooded paddocks, green crops and tidal mudflats, but prefer permanent lakes and swamps with emergent and subaquatic vegetation.

Males and females are similar in size and appearance, but males can be identified in flight by their longer necks, and when swimming, hold their necks more erect. The bird's voice can often be heard at night and is a musical honk or bugling sound.

Nests are a bulky collection of sticks and rushes generally found in fresh or brackish swamps and lakes. Between four and nine eggs are laid around late wintertime. The eggs are pale green, becoming paler through the incubation period. Incubation takes about 40 days, after which downy grey cygnets are hatched.

Each year, between September and February, black swans moult, becoming flightless. They often gather on open waterways in their thousands.

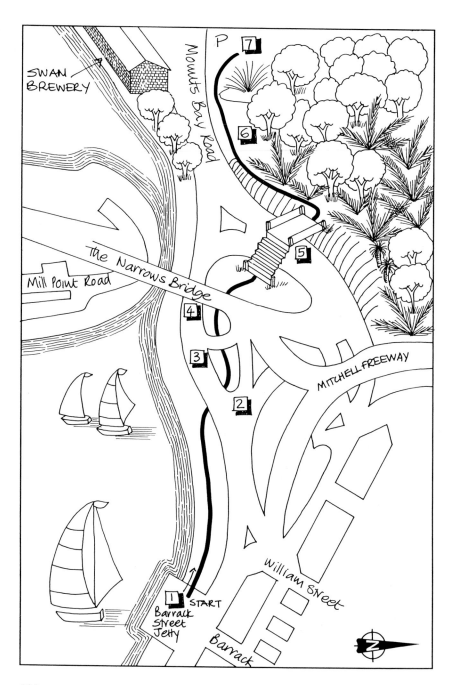

SWAN BREWERY

Mounts Bay Road

P

7

6

5

The Narrows Bridge

Mill Point Road

4

3

2

MITCHELL FREEWAY

William Street

1 START

Barrack Street Jetty

Barrack

124

Four Seasons Trail

34

Length: *5.2 kilometres return*
Grade: *2*
Walk time: *2 hours (with stops at information stations)*

This trail features information stations, which are changed according to the season (hence the name), fitness equipment, benches and good views of the river. It begins at Barrack Street Jetty and finishes at Kennedy Fountain near the old Swan Brewery.

1   Head west from Barrack Street Jetty along Riverside Drive. There are good views across the river to South Perth and along to the Narrows Bridge. Kings Park can be seen rising above the riverside beyond the Narrows.
2   Turn right into the first underpass, then first left and walk through the Narrows interchange.
3   Walk past lakes then through next underpass.
4   Turn left and walk under the Narrows Bridge towards the footbridge.
5   Cross the footbridge over Mounts Bay Road, viewing the escarpment of Kings Park. Turn left after crossing the bridge.
6   Follow the path below the escarpment south-west along Mounts Bay Road. Here you can see a variety of vegetation types.
7   Kennedy Fountain is set adjacent to a small picnic area opposite the old Swan Brewery. The fountain was Perth's first public water supply and was erected in 1861 by Governor A E Kennedy. From here you may choose to return along the same route or cross Mounts Bay Road (taking care to avoid busy traffic) and follow the footpath along the river's edge to Barrack Street Jetty.

Tracy Churchill

Where is it?: *Perth City on the north shore of Perth Water.*
Travelling time: *5 minutes from Perth GPO.*
Facilities: *Parking and toilets at Barrack Street Jetty, BBQs and parking at Kennedy Fountain.*
On-site information: *Trailhead sign and 'Four Seasons' interpretive panels along route.*
Best season: *All year.*

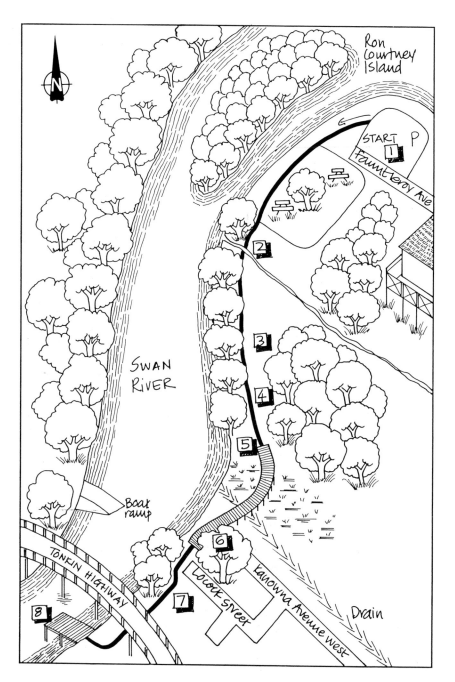

N

Ron
Courtney
Island

START P
1
Fauntleroy Ave

2

3

4

SWAN
RIVER

5

Boat
ramp

6

TONKIN HIGHWAY

8

7

Locock Street

Kanowna Avenue West

Drain

Garvey Park Riverside Walk

35

Length: *2.5 kilometres return*
Grade: *1 (accessible to wheelchairs)*
Walk time: *1 hour*

This pleasant riverside walk passes through grassland, sheoak woodland and samphire swamp. Birdlife is abundant in the woodlands and there are many varieties of waterbirds along the river banks and in the swamp area. The pathway has a bitumen surface and is ideal for wheelchairs, prams and strollers.

1   Proceed downstream from Garvey Park, with its playground and shaded picnic area set among flooded gums and overlooking Ron Courtney Island.
2   As you cross a creek the path winds into a small grove of sheoaks. Here, there are magpies, willy wagtails, galahs, little corellas and a variety of waterbirds.
3   Along this stretch, the river's edge is lined with sheoaks, reeds and sedges. On the east side of the track is an open grassland with flooded gums beyond.
4   The pathway turns away from the river's edge and winds through the edge of a dense sheoak woodland. Here, there is an abundance of birds including white-faced herons and 'twenty-eight' parrots.
5   As the vegetation changes to samphire swamp, a boardwalk elevates the pathway over the water. This area is home to many waterbirds, including egrets, grebes and herons. Snakes are likely in warmer months.
6   At the end of the boardwalk is a very large flooded gum with creepers climbing in the lower branches. From here there are excellent views upstream and across the river to Claughton Reserve. If you look under the road bridge you can see the tall buildings of Perth's city skyline.
7   Just before the bridge is a small grove of olive trees.
8   Walking under the bridge you will come to a small jetty, from where you can observe passing boats or waterbirds. Retrace your steps to Garvey Park.

John and Joel Hunter

Where is it?: *11 km east of Perth on Fauntleroy Avenue.*
Travelling time: *20 minutes via Great Eastern Highway.*
Facilities: *Wood BBQs, tables, playground, carpark, toilets, shop/cafe.*
On-site information: *None*
Best season: *Spring for birds and flowers, summer, autumn.*

Kings Park Scarp Track   **36**

Length: *3.6 kilometres return*
Grade: *2*
Walk time: *1 hour 45 minutes*

There are many walktrails through Kings Park, but this one was chosen because it offers views of the river as well as passing through native bush and landscaped areas of the park. The first part of the walk is quiet with fewer people, whereas you will encounter tourists and other sightseers after passing the War Memorial.

1   Starting from the lower carpark on Forrest Drive you are greeted by broad expansive views of the Swan River, the yachts in Matilda Bay and the city skyline. Head east along the track set high above Mounts Bay Road. Vegetation along this section includes Geraldton wax, kangaroo paws, banksias and dryandras.
2   A seat overlooking the Narrows Bridge, South Perth, Perth Water, the city skyline and, in the distance, the Darling Scarp.
3   A seat set in a quiet grove of eucalypts. Here you can watch the activities on the river. The Old Swan Brewery can be seen below through the trees.
4   Rotunda, old naval guns and a memorial to Mrs Bessie Rischbieth OBE, JP. Again, there are panoramic views from the city in the east through to the suburbs of Applecross and Attadale in the west.
5   Here, there is a beautiful view down the scarp. At the first fork in the bitumen path there is an optional path down to the Kennedy Fountain and adjacent picnic site, but remember you will have to walk back up the scarp!
6   The State War Memorial is set high above the Narrows overlooking Perth and surrounding waters. There are manicured gardens and a number of other memorials and dedicated trees.
7   The Queen Victoria Memorial. Walkers will notice a stark contrast between this and the first part of the walk. This section features manicured gardens and an avenue of lemon-scented gums, planted in 1938.
8   The 10th Light Horse Memorial. Close by is a spicnic area with barbecues.
9   This is the main gateway to Kings Park. There is an information shelter on the city side of Fraser Avenue. Look back from here to get impressive view of the lemon-scented gum. Retrace your steps to the start.

James Harrower, Pauline Kozadinos and Jacqueline Pontré

Where is it?: *4 km from the city centre on Forrest Drive.*
Travelling time: *15 minutes via Mounts Bay Road, Kings Park Avenue and Park Road.*
Facilities: *BBQs, restaurant, kiosk, toilets, carparks at various places in the park.*
On-site information: *Information booth on Fraser Avenue.*
Best season: *All year, spring for wildflowers.*

'TWENTY-EIGHT' PARROT

The 'twenty-eight' parrot is a subspecies of the Port Lincoln parrot. The normal call of the Port Lincoln is a whistling *kwink-kwing*. However, many birds around Perth emit a trisyllabic call with a rising inflection at the end that resembles the words 'twenty-eight', hence the name. Other differences include a pronounced red frontal band above the beak, larger size and heavier bill.

'Twenty-eight' parrots eat seeds, fruit, nuts, berries, nectar, blossoms, buds, insects and insect larvae. They have a strong liking for eucalyptus seeds, especially those of the marri (*Eucalyptus calophylla*).

At the start of the breeding season, pairs of parrots inspect hollows in living or dead eucalypt trees. When a nest site has been chosen, the pair defend it vigorously while the hollow is prepared for nesting. Between four and seven (usually five) eggs are laid and incubation takes about 19 days.

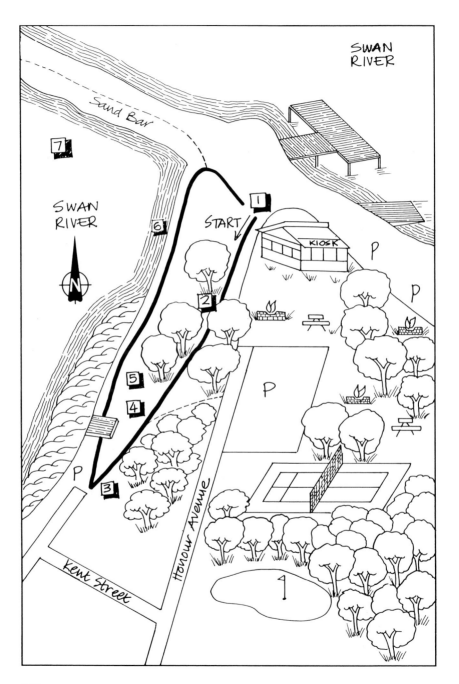

Point Walter Walk

37

Length: *2 kilometres loop (plus a kilometre return walk along the sandbar)*
Grade: *1*
Walk time: *1 hour 20 minutes*

This short but enjoyable walk is an added attraction to the already excellent family facilities at Point Walter. It provides endless vistas over the Swan River and, in parts, is teeming with birdlife. Migratory waders, such as sandpipers, stints, plovers and godwits, can be seen on or around the sandbar. Vegetation includes, tuart, marri, jarrah, peppermint and parrotbush.

1   Starting near the kiosk, there are views upstream along the river and across to the tall buildings of Perth's central business district. From here, walk uphill along Honour Avenue to the start of a dual-use cycle/walk track on your right.
2   This section of the walk is through enclosed bushland of eucalypts and low shrubs. Keep your eyes open for birds, skinks and mice.
3   When you reach the dual-use track at Blackwall Reach Parade, turn around and head back along the tra,ck taking the walktrail to the left and following cliff top. Dolphins can sometimes be seen frolicking in the river.
4   Along the cliffs is a lookout from which you can see the river clearly downstream and across to Chidley Point, Mosman Bay and Freshwater Bay.
5   The track descends close to the water's edge and looking back you can see along the foot of the cliffs.
6   On this section of the walk, the track follows either the water's edge or the path five metres above the high water mark. There are constant long-distance views over the river and its surrounds.
7   This part of the walk is optional. It takes you along the sandbar and gives excellent views both upstream and downstream.

Allan Wicks

Where is it?: *9 km south of Perth via Canning Highway and Point Walter Road.*
Travelling time: *20 minutes from Perth.*
Facilities: *BBQs, kiosk, playground, toilets, carpark, bike racks, safe swimming beach, boat ramp.*
On-site information: *None.*
Best season: *All year.*

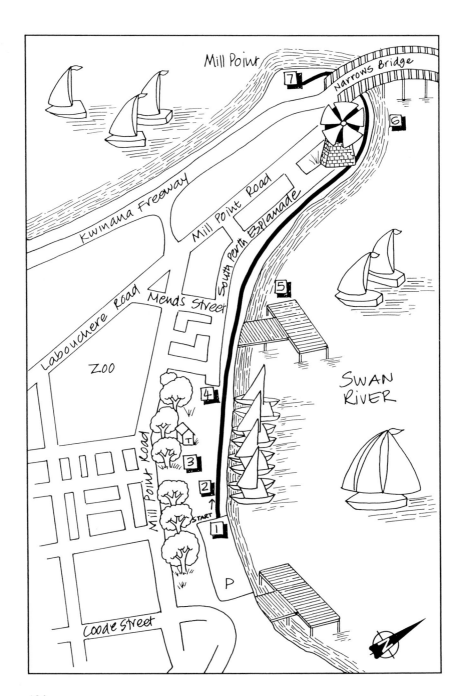

134

South Perth Foreshore

38

Length: *3.5 kilometres return*
Grade: *1*
Walk time: *1 hour 20 minutes*

This walk provides excellent views across Perth Water to the city and, near the end of the walk, across Melville Water to Kings Park and Matilda Bay.

1   Starting at the carpark at the foreshore end of Coode Street, you will find picnic shelters from which there are good views of the city. Catamarans can be hired during the summer months. Walk east from here.
2   A few minutes along the walk is a plaque commemorating the re-enactment of Sir James Stirling's landing.
3   To the left of here is an area of paperbark trees and swamp with a raised, timber-decked walkway.
4   Toilets and pergola.
5   Ferry jetty with service to Barrack Street, playground, carpark.
6   The Old Mill, by the side of the freeway on Point Belches, is the oldest surviving physical link with the pioneering days of the Swan River Colony. It was built by William Kernot Shenton and, together with the site and surrounding outbuildings, was declared a State Public Recreation Reserve in 1932. A small fee is charged for entry to the Old Mill (check opening times).
7   Continue along the river edge and under the Narrows Bridge to Mill Point. From here there are good views of Kings Park, the Old Swan Brewery, the Royal Perth Yacht Club in Matilda Bay and the South Perth Yacht Club near the Canning River. At weekends, Melville water is a mass of colourful sails and spinnakers. During the summer, parasailing is available from Mill Point. Return to the start along the same route.

Ray Bailey

Where is it?: *North end of Coode Street, South Perth.*
Travelling time: *10 minutes from Perth.*
Facilities: *Picnic tables at start of walk; restaurants, cafes and shops in Mends Street.*
On-site information: *None.*
Best season: *All year. Summer for catamarans and parasailing.*

The South   Walks 39 - 52

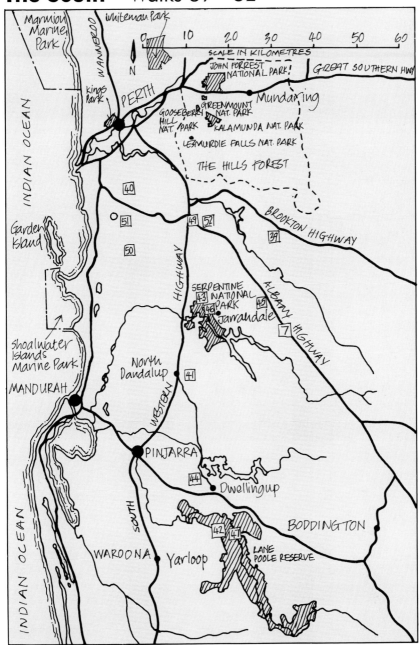

Abyssinia Rock 39

Length: *12 kilometres return*
Grade: *3*
Walk time: *5-6 hours*

The trail features jarrah woodlands, with thickets of teatree and flooded gum in the gullies, and leads to a large granite outcrop that contains a variety of plant life. Take some time to explore the rock, keeping an eye out for lizards that may be sunning themselves. Take care not to stand on the sensitive mosses as they are very slow to regenerate. Much of this walk is in Disease Risk Area, which is quarantined to help prevent the introduction and spread of dieback disease. Please ensure your boots or shoes are clean and please do not stray from the track.

1   Start at the intersection between the Brookton Highway and Bibbulmun walk track (look for powerline crossing the highway). Follow the Bibbulmun Track markers (yellow triangles with 'Waugal' symbol) south.
2   Meander down to the first gully. Along this section you will see evidence of logging and firewood cutting. Much of the bush has been thinned to promote growth and to establish regeneration (jarrah and marri seedling).
3   At this point you will notice a change in the vegetation from jarrah woodland to a scrub/heathland. This lower valley becomes too moist during the winter months for jarrah and marri to survive. Take a left turn at the 'T' junction.
4   Here you will see a water hole, which was built to provide water for fire-fighting. This type of woodland is very flammable and care must be taken when lighting a campfire or disposing of cigarette butts. A little further along, take a right turn at the totem sign. Follow the track up to Abyssinia Rock.
5   Abyssinia Rock contains a variety of plant life ranging from small mosses and liverworts to hakea shrubs and large sheoaks (*Casuarina* spp.). Adjacent to the rock is a camping site with toilets and water. Follow the Bibbulmun Track markers back to Brookton Highway.

Andy Darbyshire and Peter Gibson

Where is it?: *60 km south-east of Perth along Brookton Highway.*
Travelling time: *1 hour.*
Facilities: *Carpark at start, campsite, water and toilets at Abyssinia Rock.*
On-site information: *Yellow Bibbulmun Track markers.*
Best season: *All year except after rain when ground is wet.*

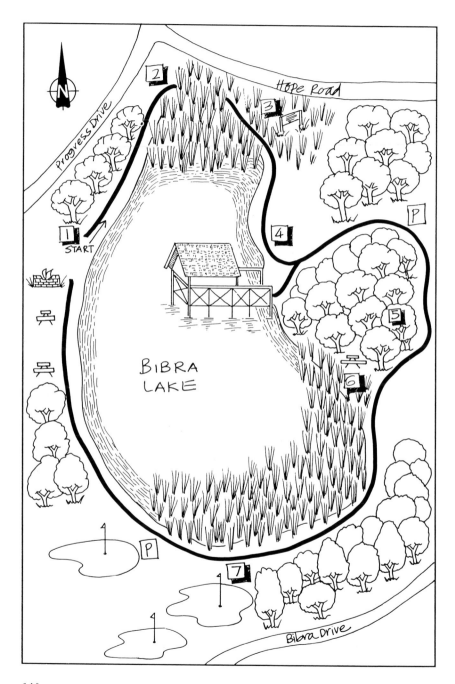

START

BIBRA LAKE

Progress Drive

Hope Road

Bibra Drive

N

1
2
3
4
5
6
7

P
P

Bibra Lake Walk

40

Length: *6 kilometres loop*
Grade: *1*
Walk time: *2 hours*

The lake and its surrounds are an outstanding refuge for birds. Waterbirds, including occasional spoonbills, inhabit the lake and surrounding reed beds. On the western side of the lake are many semi-tame birds including black swans, coots, purple swamphens and ducks. The paperbarks, flooded gums and adjoining bush vegetation attract many bush birds. The dual-use walk/cycle track is suitable for wheelchairs, prams and strollers.

1   Starting at the picnic area, the first part of the walk passes along a grassed area with some paperbarks and flooded gums.
2   Here, the reed beds become thicker and the paperbarks overhang the pathway, forming a tunnel.
3   Signs indicating the presence of snakes. Walkers should beware of snakes when walking in or near any wetland or native bush area.
4   Situated at the end of a wooden pier, well beyond the fringing paperbarks, the bird hide makes it possible for you to watch waterbirds and waders. After heavy rains, the lake's water level rises and can make the bird hide inaccessible.
5   The pathway skirts around a large area of old cultivation, which has reverted to introduced grasses and a selection of planted native trees and shrubs. This area attracts a wide variety of birds, including the chestnut-breasted manikin, a species not usually found in the South West.
6   As the path winds back to the lakeside, there is a small picnic area where you can relax and observe the wildlife.
7   This section, running back to the main picnic area, has been grassed and planted with ornamental trees.

Stacey Strickland

Where is it?: *18 km south of Perth on Progress Drive.*
Travelling time: *30 minutes via Kwinana Freeway and Hope Road.*
Facilities: *BBQs, playground, carparks, toilets.*
On-site information: *None.*
Best season: *Spring, summer, early autumn.*

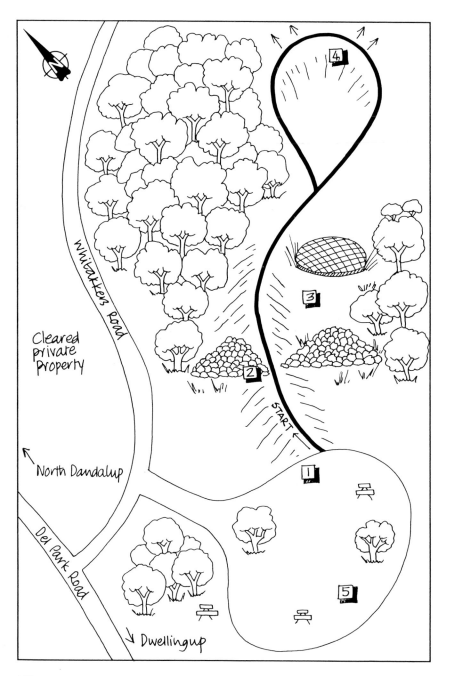

N

Whitakers Road

Cleared
private
Property

North Dandalup

Del Park Road

Dwellingup

START

1

2

3

4

5

142

Goldmine Hill

41

Length: *400 metres return*
Grade: *2*
Walk time: *15 minutes*

Although this is quite a short walk, it has been included because of its interesting features and proximity to the popular Goldmine Hill picnic site. It affords good views of the Peel Inlet and Swan Coastal Plain. Along the walk is a diversity of vegetation including salmon white gum, wandoo, and dwarf mountain marri.

1 The trailhead sign (north-east side of the carpark). From here, the trail leads up a steep, slippery incline.
2 Mullock heap. This shows the different rocks that were dug from the mineshaft as miners dug for gold.
3 Mineshaft. The shaft, which is covered by a grill, is approximately 7.5 metres deep. No gold was found in the area.
4 Lookout. Good views of the Peel Inlet and Swan Coastal Plain.
5 Picnic area. Good for fossicking with evidence of prospecting.

John Hanel

Where is it?: *65 km south of Perth via South-West Highway, Del Park Road and Whittaker Road.*
Travelling time: *1 hour 30 minutes.*
Facilities: *BBQs and carpark.*
On-site information: *Trailhead sign.*
Best season: *All year.*

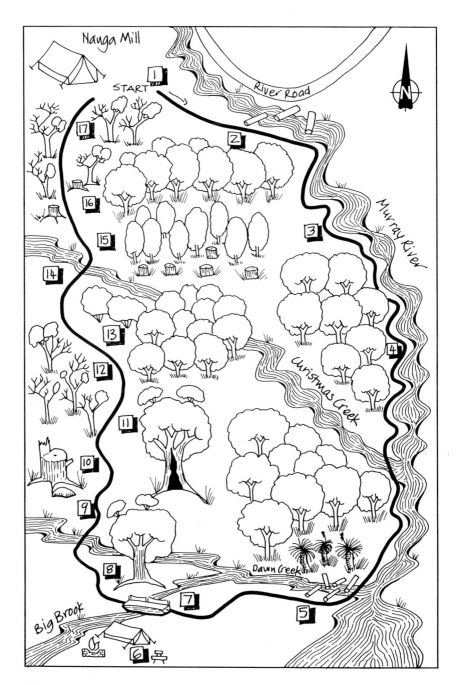

King Jarrah Track

42

Lane Poole Reserve

Length: *18 kilometres loop*
Grade: *3*
Walk time: *5 hours*

The highlight of this walk is the 'king' jarrah, a 250-year-old tree. Much of the track runs along the Murray River, and for those wishing to take their time and make a weekend of the walk, there is a campsite roughly mid-way along the track.

1   The track begins at the old Nanga Mill townsite. A campsite has now been established there in a grove of tall pines.
2   A detour off the track takes you to the Stringers, a small picnic and camping site by the Murray River with canoe-launching facilities and swimming holes. Some old bridge stringers are visible in the water.
3   An old logging railway formation with cuttings and old bridge sites.
4   Here, various reference trees (numbered trees to allow foresters to accurately locate their position in the bush) can be seen.
5   Remains of an old railway bridge.
6   Campsite with barbecue rings and toilet is approximately 200 metres off the track to the south.
7   A log bridge takes you over Big Brook.
8   The 'king' jarrah tree.
9   Dawn Creek - has good water in winter and spring.
10 A very large, old axe and crosscut stump with evidence of board notches is visible here.
11 A large burnt-out, hollow jarrah tree.
12 Here, the track skirts a large dieback-infected area. Some trees along the track have been blown over, exposing the underlying rock.
13 The track passes through dense prickly thickets of waterbush.
14 Christmas Creek is a small seasonal creek. Birdsong and frog calls can be heard at appropriate times of the year.
15 An even-aged regrowth forest with numerous large stumps and old logging debris.
16 A very colourful acacia grows here and flowers in the spring.
17 Just before returning to Nanga Mill, the trail passes through a very badly affected dieback area.

Matthew Reynolds

Where is it?: *Nanga Mill, 13 km south of Dwellingup along Nanga Road.*
Travelling time: *2 hours 30 minutes from Perth.*
Facilities: *BBQs, tables, toilets, campsite.*
On-site information: *Signs on access road and at trailhead, yellow markers along the route.*
Best season: *Spring for wildflowers, summer.*

THE JARRAH FOREST

The jarrah forest extends from the south coast almost to New Norcia, about 125 kilometres north of Perth. It is bounded on the east by the line of annual rainfall of about 600 millimetres. In the northern part of its range it is found on laterite soils on the Darling Range and occasionally in the sandy soils of the coastal plain.

Jarrah (*Eucalyptus marginata*) has dark grey or reddish brown bark with deep vertical groves. It grows to about 40 metres tall on the richest and best watered soils of the Darling Range, but seldom reaches more than 15 metres on poorer sandy soils.

Jarrah forms extensive forests, where they grow about half-a-centimetre in diameter a year and can live more than 400 years. Few other trees occur within these forests, except on deeper soils or river banks. The trees are generally widely spaced with an open crown allowing light to pass through to the forest floor. It is a beautiful forest all year round, but particularly during the spring, when its understorey of shrubs and herbs bursts into flower.

Jarrah is a good honey-yielding species and jarrah pollen is considered to be highly nutritious. The jarrah forests and coastal stands yield fairly large quantities of a medium amber, nutty-flavoured honey.

START

Gooralong Brook

Kitty's Gorge Road

148

Kitty's Track

43

Length: *4.5 kilometres loop*
Grade: *4*
Walk time: *2 hours*

This walk passes down the Darling Scarp into the Gooralong Brook valley to a gauging station. It returns along the brook and through jarrah forest, giving views to the ocean. It also features interesting vegetation on the granite slopes.

1   Starting from the carpark, cross the bridge at Gooralong Brook. The brook flows all year round. From here, head south on the western side of the brook.
2   About 200 metres from the start of the walk, several side tracks lead down to the brook giving pleasant views of the pools.
3   Occasional gullies, flowing over the track only during the winter.
4   Granite outcrops are visible on both sides of the brook. The stunted flora in these areas has adapted to the poor soil and harsh conditions.
5   WAWA water gauging station. This weir and wall is an active measuring site for water quality and quantity. Cross the brook at this point.
6   Continue south, on the east side of the brook, along the weir access track.
7   After about 1.5 kilometres, the track takes a swing to the east and then north. Follow the direction markers to the top of the ridge.
8   Leave the access track and go north along the top of the ridge, following the markers.
9   Winding through the bush you will have excellent views to the ocean around Mandurah.
10 Continue until you arrive at another track. Turn left and head for the Gooralong Pine Plantation.
11 When you reach the Pine Plantation, walk downhill to the carpark and picnic facilities.

Andy Darbyshire

Where is it?: *Gooralong, 50 km south of Perth via Jarrahdale.*
Travelling time: *1 hour 10 minutes from Perth.*
Facilities: *BBQs, carpark, toilets.*
On-site information: *Display shelter at Gooralong, markers along track.*
Best season: *Spring for wildflowers.*

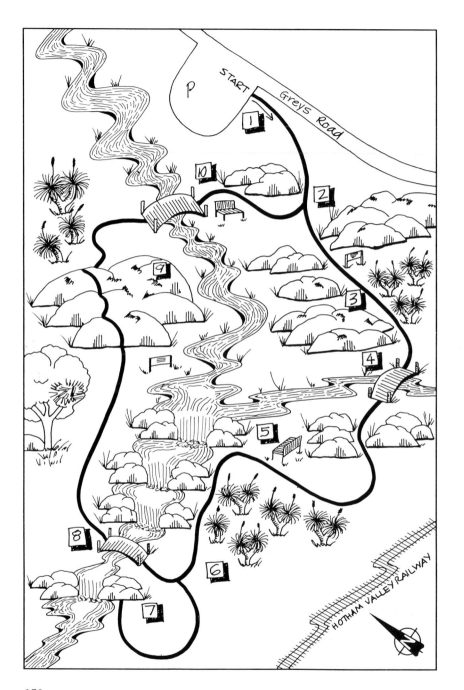

Marrinup Falls

44

Length: *1.5 kilometres loop*
Grade: *1*
Walk time: *45 minutes*

This walk takes you through a variety of vegetation and along Marrinup Brook to the falls, returning on opposite bank.

1 Trail begins at the southern end of the carpark.
2 A large granite outcrop covered in moss lichens and fungi is on the left of the trail at the junction of the return loop. Looking west, in trees on top of the hill, you may see a wedge-tailed eagle's nest.
3 Trail winds down over rocks and past an interpretive sign to Marrinup Brook. Many, large, multi-headed blackboys can be seen in this area.
4 A small log bridge crosses Marrinup Brook and the trail turns right towards the Falls.
5 A seat is provided along this section. The trail then passes a series of waterfalls before reaching the junction with the return loop.
6 At this point, a spur leads off to the left and runs down to the main falls.
7 Main falls and pool. Brown quail may sometime be seen here. Return to point 6 and turn left along the return loop.
8 A small log footbridge crosses to the opposite bank of Marrinup Brook.
9 The track climbs uphill past interpretive signs and crosses a large granite outcrop before turning right to cross an unnamed creek.
10 A small causeway crosses the creek. At this point there is a log seat where you can rest for a while. The trail then leads back up to join the outward loop at point 2, before turning left towards the carpark.

John Hanel

Where is it?: *100 km south of Perth via Williams Road, east from Dwellingup, and Grey Road.*
Travelling time: *2 hours 15 minutes.*
Facilities: *Carpark. (Tavern, shops, petrol etc. in Dwellingup.)*
On-site information: *Interpretive signs along the route.*
Best season: *All year, winter and spring for waterfalls and wildflowers.*

Mt. Vincent

6
5
4
3
2
1

Sullivan Rock

Forest track
Bibbulmun track

ALBANY HIGHWAY

SULLIVAN ROCK

P

BIBBULMUN TRACK

START
ALBANY HIGHWAY

N

Mt Vincent via Sullivan Rock

45

Monadnocks Conservation Park

Length: *7 kilometres return*
Grade: *4*
Walk time: *2 hours 30 minutes*

This trail features scenic views and granite outcrops, called 'monadnocks' by local Aborigines. It is particularly rewarding if taken during wildflower season. Many birds can be seen: ravens and grey currawongs near the highway; scarlet robins, grey fantails and splendid fairy wrens in the forest; and wedgetail eagles in the sky above Mt Vincent.

1   After parking at the picnic area, cross Albany Highway following the Bibbulmun Track up Sullivan Rock. Pegs set into the rock mark the trail and should be strictly followed. A variety of plantlife exists on the rock and much of it is very sensitive. If walked on, most of the plants will die. Mt Cooke can be seen to the south-east.
2   From Sullivan Rock, you leave the Bibbulmun Track (yellow markers) taking a turn to the right. Continue on into an area of mature jarrah and marri forest.
3   As you cross the small ridge you will see many old stumps of trees cut by axe and cross-cut saw. On the right is a stump that still has an original peg in it.
4   The track runs to the right of a large granite outcrop.
5   Here the track passes through a thick stand of hakeas and is partly overgrown. At the fork, take the lower track. If you look at the horizon to the north-west you can just see Alcoa's Jarrahdale mine clearing.
6   To the east of here there is a small lookout on a spur track. Yellow direction markers are fixed to a tree at this point. Take the left-hand track.
7   At the summit there is a cairn (pile of rocks). Looking north you can see Mt Cuthbert and slightly east on the horizon is Mt Dale. Retrace your steps to the picnic area.

Ken Wheeler and Grant Hansen

Where is it?: *Sullivan Rock, 65 km south of Perth on the Albany Highway.*
Travelling time: *1 hour 30 minutes.*
Facilities: *Picnic area, BBQ, carpark.*
On-site information: *Trailhead sign, some markers along route.*
Best season: *Autumn, winter, spring for wildflowers.*

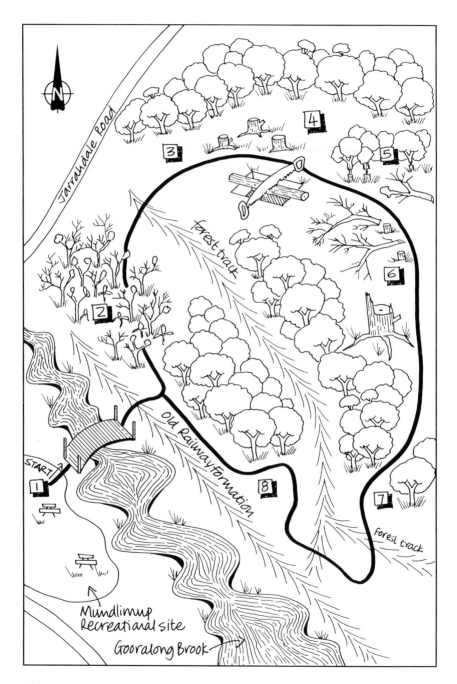

Mundlimup Trail

46

Length: *3.2 kilometres loop*
Grade: *3*
Walk time: *1 hour*

This trail features a history of logging and silviculture, and passes through a fine example of northern jarrah forest.

1   Starting from the Mundlimup Recreation Site, cross the bridge over the creek to an old railway formation. Turn right, proceed about 50 metres and turn left.
2   About 100 metres from the railway formation is a small dieback-infected area. Here you can see the devastation the disease can bring in fresh banksia and jarrah deaths.
3   On this part of the trail you will see evidence of old logging operations.
4   This old sawpit was used prior to the 1950s for milling logs. Using a two-handed saw, one man stood on top of a log while another stood in the pit beneath, and together they sawed rough planks of wood - a primitive method by today's standards.
5   Crossing a forest track, you will see old trees that have been ringbarked. This was a method used to kill non-viable trees and promote the growth of more valuable crop trees.
6   A little further on you will see a large stump with a trail marker attached. The tree was felled with axe and crosscut saw. Often, trees were cut high to reduce the diameter and/or to get above any defects. To cut a tree high up, axemen stood on pegs attached to the sides of the tree. The notches that would have taken such pegs can still be seen in the stump.
7   Follow the forest track for a few hundred metres then branch off to the left through more open jarrah woodland, keeping an eye open for the trail markers.
8   The track leads back onto the old railway formation. Follow this back to the recreation site.

Peter Gibson

Where is it?: *55 km south of Perth via Jarrahdale Road and Balmoral Road.*
Travelling time: *1 hour from Perth.*
Facilities: *BBQs, carpark.*
On-site information: *Directional signs along the trail.*
Best season: *Autumn, spring for wildflowers.*

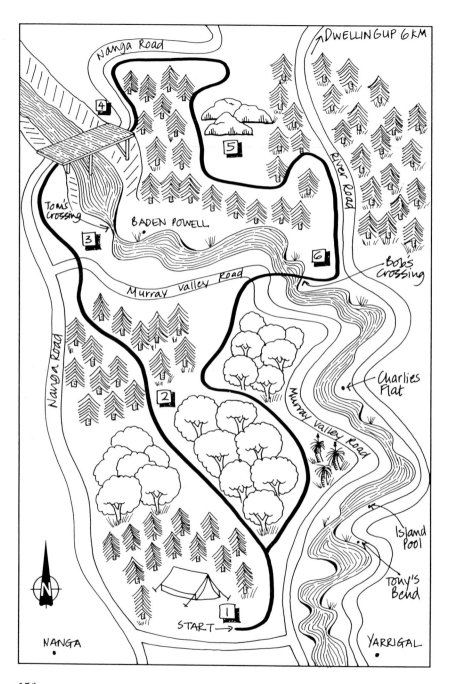

156

Nanga Circuit

47

Lane Poole Reserve

Length: *17 kilometres loop*
Grade: *2*
Walk time: *5 hours 30 minutes*

This is one of the longest walks in the book and, at a leisurely pace, makes a pleasant day's walk.

It is best to get an early start or plan the walk as part of a weekend and camp at one of several campsites in Lane Poole Reserve.

1   The trail starts at the Nanga Mill campsite, which has been established in a grove of tall pines.
2   The clear-felled area gives excellent views of the surrounding forest.
3   Tom's Crossing - good views of the river rapids and permanent freshwater stream.
4   The trail crosses the Murray River on a large trestle bridge.
5   From the top of this granite outcrop you can see over the pine plantation to the river and trestle bridge, and over surrounding bushland.
6   Cross the Murray River again at Bob's Crossing. This is a pleasant and tranquil area. From here, follow the track along an old railway formation through jarrah trees back to Nanga Mill.

John Hanel

Where is it?: *Nanga Mill, 13 km south of Dwellingup along Nanga Road.*
Travelling time: *2 hours 30 minutes from Perth.*
Facilities: *BBQs, tables, toilets, campsite.*
On-site information: *Red 'Waugal' directional signs along trail.*
Best season: *Spring for wildflowers.*

Oakley Falls

48

Length: *1 kilometre circular*
Grade: *5*
Walk time: *30 minutes*

This is a short, but interesting, walk with opportunities to view the falls from several vantage points.

1   The picnic area has barbecues and tables set beneath marri trees and among many scarp plant species including winged wattle and fucia grevillea.
2   A large flat granite outcrop covered in a variety of mosses and lichens.
3   The dam wall was originally built in 1939 to provide water for steam locomotives at Pinjarra.
4   The trail leads between two large overhanging granite boulders
5   A short spur to the left of the main trail leads to a large flat granite rock. From here you can see Alcoa's refinery below.
6   Wooden walkway. Leads over the top of the falls with excellent view of the falls and the dam.
7   The trail crosses the old pipeline which carried the water to railway.
8   Just beyond the pipeline, another spur to the left of the main track leads to a viewing platform. This part of the trail leads down through the trees and is quite steep in places. Along the trail are good stands of salmon white gum. From the viewing platform there are excellent views of the base of the falls.
9   From here it is possible to gain access to the dam wall. Anglers often use this area to fish for introduced rainbow trout. (Normal, current fishing regulations apply.)
10 The trail leads back over granite outcrops overlooking the dam. This is a good area for viewing orchids.
11 A small footbridge crosses Oakley Brook to finish at the carpark.

John Hanel

Where is it?: *120 km from Perth via the South West Highway, Adelaide Road and Scarp Road.*
Travelling time: *1 hour 25 minutes.*
Facilities: *BBQs, toilets, carpark.*
On-site information: *Trailhead sign, interpretive signs.*
Best season: *Spring for wildflowers, winter for waterfall.*

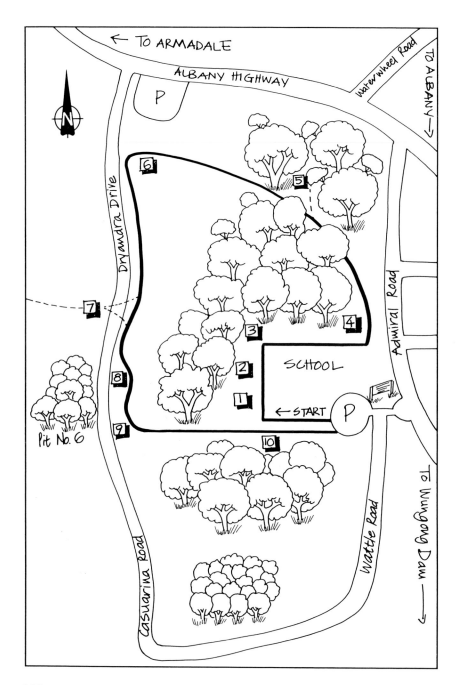

Robin Ramble

49

Bungendore Park

Length: *3 kilometres loop*
Grade: *4*
Walk time: *1 hour 30 minutes*

This is one in a series of walks in Bungendore Park near Armadale. The walk winds through sheoak trees and dense parrotbush, where western spinebills and new holland honeyeaters search for nectar.

1 The walk starts at the carpark just south of Emmaus School. Follow the yellow dots into jarrah woodland.
2 An interpretive totem by the side of the trail. Snottygobbles (*Persoonia* spp.) and bull banksias (*Banksia grandis*) nearby.
3 At the junction with Spinebill Stroll (marked by red squares), there is a change of vegetation to sheoaks.
4 The track turns left into an area of parrotbush (*Dryandra sessilis*).
5 Junction with Whistler Walk (marked by red diamonds).
6 At the junction with Dryandra Drive there are many grevilleas and hibbertias.
7 Open views can be had at the junction with Honeyeater Hike (marked by yellow squares).
8 The rehabilitation project at gravel pit No.6 began in June 1987. Parrotbush has revegetated naturally, whereas marri and other trees have been planted.
9 This point marks the junction of Dryandra Drive with Casuarina Road and Spinebill Stroll. Turn left and head east.
10 Arrive back at the carpark.

Terry Hales

Where is it?: *31 km from Perth off Admiral Road.*
Travelling time: *1 hour 10 minutes from Perth via Albany Highway.*
Facilities: *Carpark.*
On-site information: *Signs on access road, at trailhead and along trail.*
Best season: *Autumn, winter, spring for wildflowers.*

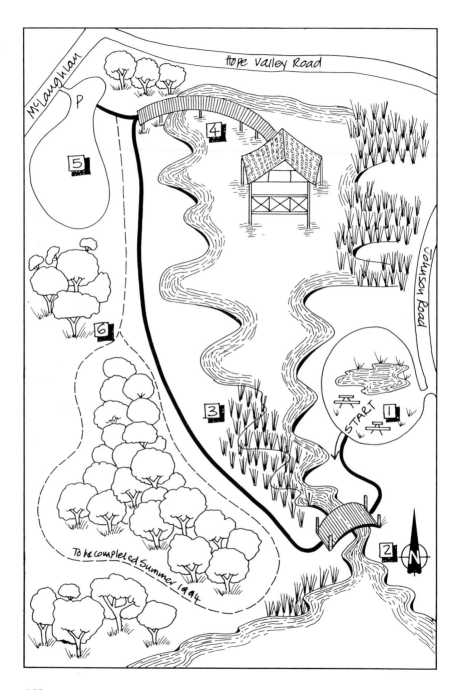

The Spectacles Walktrail

50

Length: *5 kilometres return*
Grade: *1 (accessible be wheelchair).*
Walk time: *2 hours*

The walktrail is part of a joint CALM-Alcoa project in this important wetland area. The trail features paperbark groves, banksia woodland, wildflowers (in season) and a 100 metre boardwalk to a bird hide. A nature trail with interpretive panels on the theme of pollination will be completed in summer 1994-95.

1   Johnson Road Picnic Area overlooks reed beds and open water.
2   The bridge over the channel is the link between the two 'eyes' of The Spectacles. Water flows all year and the area attracts birds, frogs, insects and reptiles. There is a bench and rest area.
3   The valley. This largely open area is being revegetated. Thousands of indigenous plants can be seen in their protective enclosures. This is a transition zone between the woodland and wetland and the trail winds through both. Benches and bicycle racks are provided and views are available to the wetland basin.
4   Pleasant enclosed paperbark wetland with a boardwalk to the open water bird hide. Provides visitors with the opportunity to experience remoteness in a natural area. Here you could see birds, insects, the occasional snake and other reptiles and amphibians.
5   The McLaughlan Road entrance with carpark and trailhead information shelter in banksia woodland. Return to Johnson Road Picnic Area.
6   **Optional Nature Trail (due to be completed in summer 1994-95).**
    This superb 3 kilometre loop trail on gentle terrain passes through remnant jarrah-banksia coastal vegetation. There are views to the wetland and benches along a well-defined and interpreted path. The trail focuses on the pollination process.

Richard Hammond

Where is it?: *31 km from Perth on Johnson Road.*
Travelling time: *40 minutes from Perth via Nicholson Road and Thomas Road.*
Facilities: *Picnic tables, carpark.*
On-site information: *Trailhead signs, information shelter.*
Best season: *All year, spring for wildflowers.*

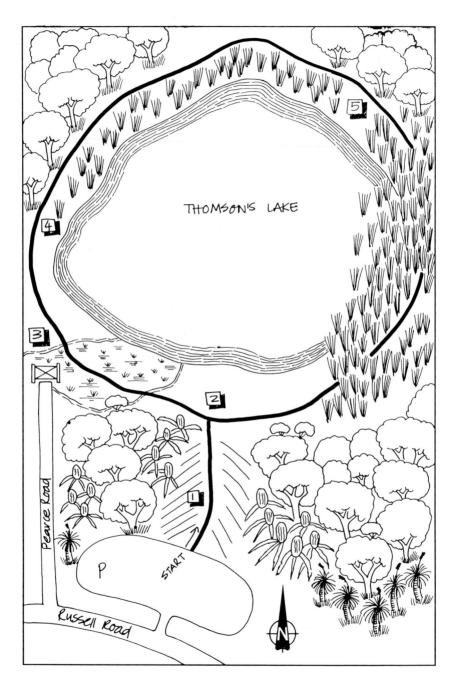

THOMSON'S LAKE

5

4

3

2

1

P

START

Pearce Road

Russell Road

N

Thomson's Lake Trail

51

Length: 5.7 kilometres loop
Grade: 4
Walk time: 3 hours

This walk features bulrushes, birds and the wetlands environment. Thomsons Lake is an important area for migratory waterbirds, especially waders. In winter there are more birds on the wetland, but parts of the trail become waterlogged. In summer the trail is drier and more accessible, but take care as snakes are more abundant.

1 From the crest of the ridge, a few metres from the carpark, there are excellent views across the lake and of the nearby jarrah-banksia woodland.
2 At the 'T' junction, turn left and proceed around the lake in a clockwise direction. Along this section are bulrushes and partial views onto the water.
3 Here, the trail passes close to the vermin-proof fence, built to help conserve wildlife, and there is a pedestrian access gate. This area can be inundated during winter.
4 Areas cleared of vegetation reflect past disturbances and current grazing by rabbits. The fence should help control this problem and allow regrowth of natural vegetation.
5 Here, the trail moves into reed beds with occasional glimpses to the lake. Wetland vegetation is more evident than on the west side and wading birds are more common during winter. Rushes can give visual protection to visitors wanting to watch the birds without disturbing them. The track along this eastern edge becomes waterlogged during winter.

Tracy Churchill

Where is it?: 34 km south of Perth. Entrance at Russell Road, between Pearse Road and Hammond Road.
Travelling time: 30 minutes from Perth via Kwinana Freeway, Forrest Road and Hammond Road.
Facilities: Carpark.
On-site information: None.
Best season: Spring, autumn.

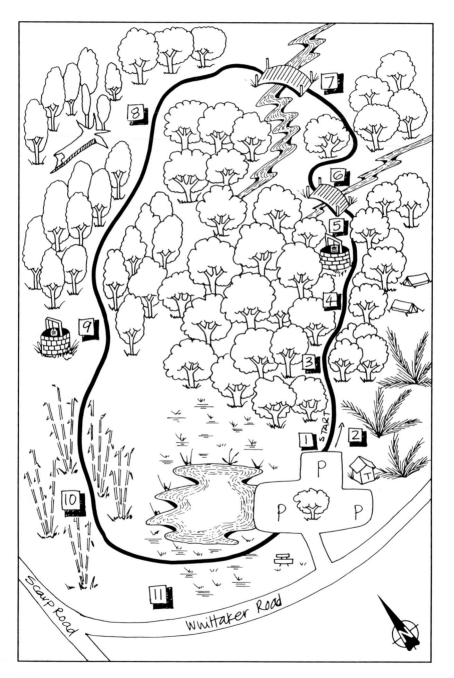

Whittakers Walktrail

52

Length: *500 metres*
Grade: *1*
Walk time: *15 minutes*

This short walk takes you through glades of introduced trees and plants that were once in the gardens of the Whittakers Mill townsite.

1   Trail begins at the north end of the carpark.
2   Huge zamias can be seen in this area to the right of the track, adjacent to the toilets.
3   Large blackbutt trees can be seen along this section of the trail.
4   The trail enters a silver birch forest, giving a glade-like feeling as these trees intertwine and create a unique experience. These, along with many other introduced species give an indication that the area was once the gardens of the old townsite.
5   Old well.
6   A small footbridge crosses the stream as the trail passes through black wattle forest.
7   A second footbridge crosses the stream near to an old steam boiler.
8   An enormous upturned black stump that now has trees sprouting from its base.
9   Another old well among a forest of introduced trees.
10 A large area of prickly pear and bamboo.
11 Before returning to the carpark, the trail passes through a wetland area supporting numerous frogs and birds.

John Hanel

Where is it?: *65 km south of Perth via South West Highway, Del Park Road and Whittaker Road.*
Travelling time: *1 hour 30 minutes.*
Facilities: *BBQs, toilets, carpark, campsite.*
On-site information: *Trailhead sign, directional signs en route.*
Best season: *All year.*

Index by name

Name	Region	Walk No.
Robin Ramble	South	49
Sixty-foot Falls Walk	Hills	9
Slippery Dip Walktrail	Hills	10
South Perth Foreshore Walk	River	38
Southell Track	Hills	11
Star Swamp Trail	North	23
The Spectacles Walktrail	South	50
Thomson's Lake Trail	South	51
Trigg Bushland Trail	North	24
Valley to Valley Walk	Hills	12
Werillyiup Trail	North	25
Whittakers Walktrail	South	52
Winjan Track	Hills	13
Wunanga Walktrail	North	26
Yaberoo Budjara Heritage Trail #1	North	27
Yaberoo Budjara Heritage Trail #5	North	28
Yanjidi Trail	North	29
Yonga Neandup Walktrail	North	30
Zamia Trail	North	31

BLACK DUCK

Index by walk length

Length(return)	Name	Region	Walk No.
5.2 km	Four Seasons Trail	River	34
5.2 km*	Yaberoo Budjara Heritage Trail #5	North	28
5.7 km	Thomson's Lake Trail	South	51
6 km	Bibra Lake Walk	South	40
7 km	Mt Cooke Walktrail	Hills	7
7 km	Mt Vincent Walktrail	South	45
7.2 km	Winjan Track	Hills	13
8 km*	Valley to Valley Walk	Hills	12
8.5 km**	Southell Track	Hills	11
8.5 km	Kingfisher Trail	North	21
10 km	Between the Bridges Walk	River	32
10.2 km	John Forrest Heritage Trail	Hills	2
✔ 10.6 km	Echidna Trail	North	15
✔ 11 km	Ghost House Walk	North	16
✔ 12 km	Little Oven Circuit	Hills	6
12 km	Abyssinia Rock Walktrail	South	39
✔ 17 km	Nanga Circuit	South	47
✔ 18 km	King Jarrah Trail	South	42

*One-way (Best walked from south to north.)
**One-way (Best walked from north to south.)

Index by ecosystem

Name	Region	Walk No.

The Forests and Woodlands of the Darling Range and Scarp

Name	Region	Walk No.
Glen Brook Trail	Hills	1
John Forrest Heritage Trail	Hills	2
Lakeside Walk	Hills	3
Lesley Nature Trail	Hills	4
Lesmurdie Falls Walktrail	Hills	5
Little Oven Circuit	Hills	6
Mt Cooke	Hills	7
Portagabra Track	Hills	8
Sixty-foot Falls Walk	Hills	9
Slippery Dip Walktrail	Hills	10
Southell Track	Hills	11
Valley to Valley Walk	Hills	12
Winjan Track	Hills	13
Blackboy Ridge Walktrail	North	14
Echidna Trail	North	15
Kangaroo Trail	North	20
Kingfisher Trail	North	21
Abyssinia Rock Walktrail	South	39
Goldmine Hill Walk	South	41
King Jarrah Trail	South	42
Kitty's Track	South	43
Marrinup Falls	South	44
Mt Vincent Walktrail	South	45
Mundlimup Trail	South	46
Nanga Circuit	South	47
Oakley Falls Walk	South	48
Robin Ramble	South	49
Whittakers Walktrail	South	52

Name	Region	Walk No.

The Woodlands of the Coastal Plain

Name	Region	Walk No.
Ghost House Walk	North	16
Goo-loorto Walktrail	North	17
Lake Joondalup Nature Trail	North	22
Star Swamp Trail	North	23
Trigg Bushland Trail	North	24
Werillyiup Trail	North	25
Wunanga Walktrail	North	26
Yaberoo Budjara Heritage Trail #1	North	27
Yaberoo Budjara Heritage Trail #5	North	28
Yanjidi Trail	North	29
Yonga Neandup Walktrail	North	30
Zamia Trail	North	31
Kings Park Scarp Track	River	36
Point Walter Walk	River	37
Thomson's Lake Trail	South	51

The Wetlands of Lakes, Rivers, Streams and Estuaries

Name	Region	Walk No.
Glen Brook Trail	Hills	1
Lakeside Walk	Hills	3
Lesmurdie Falls Walktrail	Hills	5
Sixty-foot Falls Walk	Hills	9
Slippery Dip Walktrail	Hills	10
Valley to Valley Walk	Hills	12
Ghost House Walk	North	16
Goo-loorto Walktrail	North	17
Lake Joondalup Nature Trail	North	22
Star Swamp Trail	North	23
Werillyiup Trail	North	25
Wunanga Walktrail	North	26
Yaberoo Budjara Heritage Trail #1	North	27
Yanjidi Trail	North	29
Between the Bridges Walk	River	32
Claremont Foreshore Trail	River	33
Four Seasons Trail	River	34
Garvey Park Riverside Walk	River	35
Kings Park Scarp Track	River	36

Name	Region	Walk No.
Point Walter Walk	River	37
South Perth Foreshore Walk	River	38
Bibra Lake Walk	South	40
King Jarrah Trail	South	42
Kitty's Track	South	43
Marrinup Falls	South	44
Oakley Falls Walk	South	48
The Spectacles Walktrail	South	50
Thomson's Lake Trail	South	51

The Coast and Marine Environments

Guilderton Lighthouse Trail	North	18
Iluka Foreshore Walktrail	North	19

CALM offices in Perth Outdoors

State Operations Headquarters

50 Hayman Road PO Box 104
COMO 6152
☎ (09) 334 0333 Fax: (09)334 0466

Regional Office

3044 Albany Highway
KELMSCOTT 6111
☎ (09) 390 5977 Fax: (09) 390 7059

District Offices

Dwellingup:
Banksiadale Road DWELLINGUP 6213
☎ (09) 538 1001 Fax: (09) 538 1203

Jarrahdale:
George Street JARRAHDALE 6203
☎ (09) 525 5004 Fax: (09) 525 5547

Mundaring:
Mundaring Weir Road MUNDARING 6073
☎ (09) 295 1955 Fax: (09) 295 2404

Perth:
5 Dundebar Road WANNEROO 6065
☎ (09) 405 0700 Fax: (09) 405 0777

Now it's your turn . . .

We have already begun collecting information for a second volume of *Family Walks in Perth Outdoors*. Some of the walks likely to be included are in the following places:

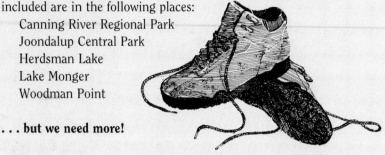

- Canning River Regional Park
- Joondalup Central Park
- Herdsman Lake
- Lake Monger
- Woodman Point

. . . but we need more!

If you have a favourite walk that you feel others would enjoy and appreciate as much as you do, please let us know. Take a photocopy of this page and send us the details.

Walk/Location   **Approx length**

_____

_____

_____

_____

_____

_____

Name _____

Address _____

_____ Telephone _____

Please send to:
More Family Walks in Perth Outdoors
Corporate Relations Division
Department of Conservation and Land Management
PO Box 104, Como 6152